Contents

Acknowledgements

This book would have been impossible to develop and complete without the individuals and institutions who helped and collaborated with me along the way. The research this work is based on started in 1999 when I undertook a project about cleaning, homes and lifestyles for Unilever Research, developed with Katie Deverell. This was followed in 2000 by a second project about laundry practice, developed with Jean Rimmer at Unilever Research and undertaken with Marie Corbin of the University of Kent as a co-researcher. These collaborations were exciting and informative and helped me develop my ideas about the sensory home.

When embarking on a project such as this a researcher is confronted with the daunting question of whether anyone will agree to be recorded on video showing an anthropologist around their private home. To contact my interviewees I worked along networks, and am grateful to everyone who put me in contact with another person who was interested in being interviewed. During the course of this research I interviewed fifty women and men each of whom shared with me their unique and personal experience of their home. I thank everyone who participated for welcoming me and making the research experience both fascinating and enjoyable. To write this book I contacted all the informants whom I could trace to ask their permission to use their interviews and if they would like their names to be changed. I have only used the interviews of those who gave their written consent.

Writing up this work has been a long process, punctuated by maternity leave and work commitments and completed during sabbatical leave from Loughborough University. I would particularly like to thank Paul Moores and Sue Stanley of Unilever Research for their support during this process. For their comments on the manuscript as it developed I am grateful to John Postill (Bremen University, Germany) and Berg's anonymous reader.

Prologue: Everyday Sensory Lives

When I began to research other people's domestic worlds the topic held a compelling contradiction for me. Exploring practices of housework and home decoration that are usually hidden or done alone I delved into a fascinating world of activities about which some of my informants had never spoken before. By simply stepping into the intimate context of a domestic world I became involved in narratives, practices and sensory experiences that were not usually available for public view. Other people's homes became almost exotic sensory spaces where others live strange lives and I often felt privileged that they had allowed me access to these parts of their worlds. Simultaneously, having lived myself in numerous homes in England and in six homes in Spain, there was something unavoidably familiar about the homes I explored. Each was framed by cultural, gendered and biographical reference points. By collaboratively exploring other people's homes with them and my video camera, I began to see each home as a creative domain, a space where each individual I interviewed could articulate her or his unique gendered self in negotiation with the sensory, social, cultural and material environment in which she or he lived. In fact, in our video interviews, each informant used her or his home as a way of representing their gendered self. Our tours of the home followed narratives structured in relation to the material physical home, which was simultaneously used as a device for self-representation.

When I interviewed Maureen in 1999 she was in her fifties and retired. Now a housewife who enjoyed her housework, she had lived in her current home for eleven years. For her, maintaining a clean and tidy home entailed constantly recreating a particular sensory environment. She told me, 'I get satisfaction out of [the housework] because as I say I like to see it clean and tidy, you know. So I like the finished article, when you look I think you get a lot of satisfaction out of it.' Olfaction was also a priority because she treated the smell of her home as an index of its cleanliness: 'I feel the house has been cleaned and it won't be cleaned if I just dusted it, as far as I'm concerned. It would need to have, to smell fresh when you go into it.' Maureen organized the burning of oils and joss sticks according to other olfactory agencies in each room. For example:

Maureen:	out in the hall I've got 2 that I put on which is a jasmine and a lily of the valley together which are nice . . .
Sarah:	What do you put in the kitchen then?
Maureen:	The one I've got, I can't think what it's called, it's a musk but it's an oil I use in there . . . yes, a sea oil. And even where the dog sleeps in the utility room . . . I even have those sticks, the joss sticks.

Her olfactory strategies constituted engagement with other agencies of the home, for example, dust, dog hair and odour, cooking odours, the mustiness of curtains and the 'smell' the house has after going away and leaving it closed up.

Maureen's narrative interwove the visual ('when you look'), olfactory ('to smell fresh') and emotional ('satisfaction'). She also described her relaxation at home in terms of sensory experience. She plays the piano, a tactile and aural experience, and knits, a tactile and rhythmic activity that should not require vision for a good knitter. Her relationship with and uses of these material objects are mediated by activities that she speaks of in terms of non-visual sensory experience. This is not to say that she would never read piano music or knitting patterns or glance down at her stitches. However the textures, sounds and smells of her home are elements that she is articulate about.

These sensory elements of home are temporary. The use of sound to create particular atmospheres of home that are expressive of both mood and self-identity and are consciously used to create moods and inspire particular activities was common amongst my informants. Music might be used to create a temporary atmosphere of self and home at particular times of the day. Smell is transient and uncontainable. As such Maureen's interactions with the sensory aspects of her home were activities or processes in which different sensory elements would participate to varying degrees at different times. For example, when she cleaned her home she played music and often listened to her *Celtic Reflections* CD, as she explained, 'it is Irish, I mean I'm not Irish, this is Irish music but I like this sort of thing, you know. I think it's just soothing, you know, and I can work better to music as well.' She sometimes varied this, also enjoying Scottish music and Gilbert and Sullivan. She left music playing in the kitchen so she could hear it 'in the background' when she cleaned upstairs, and listened to it when she ironed in the kitchen. She combined this with creating an olfactory environment by burning candles with flowery smells 'if I do my cleaning I always have that. I've always got smells, candles and whatever going':

Say if I was going to clean this morning . . . I will put them [candles or oils] on even if, because I like the smell of it myself, it's something different and I used to use the Shake n Vac but now I've got the other hoover that you're not supposed to use Shake n Vac. So I'm not using that. And that, you see, made a nice smell on the carpets. So I will have to have something to replace that smell, you know what I'm saying? That's me. So I've either got stuff that you spray on the settee and it makes a nice smell. So that's what I put in the room – the kitchen as well. Of course obviously when I'm cooking I have some [candles or oils] on the go, you know, but I don't like the smell of cooking.

The series of activities she described formed part of a wider process of olfactory transformation for Maureen. Although she 'didn't mind' the smells of detergents after using them she would always 'put a candle in or something just to finish the job off'.

Through housework Maureen consciously created an environment with a balance of sound and smell that was satisfying. She simultaneously experienced the texture and sight of domestic surfaces and objects that in some instances she transformed. In our interview Maureen's verbal descriptions separated the different sensory aspects of her experience of housework, which she connected to the dog and different material objects and technologies. This does not mean that her embodied experience of each sensory modality was necessarily singular. They combined to constitute her experience of and relationship with her environment but were separated by the linguistic metaphors through which she represented her experience.

Our interview was not simply verbal, its second half was an hour-long video interview in which Maureen showed me her home. We discussed her decorations, the rooms and objects in them (such as candles, oils, perfumes and the dog basket). Maureen showed me the material props of her sensory engagement with her home, and as we browsed around her house I also experienced smells, visions and textures she had spoken of. Video is an audio-visual rather than visual medium, and Maureen was aware of this as the video camera became part of our communication. She played a track from her CD of Celtic ballads for me, using it as a prop that was evocative of the sensory atmosphere she did her housework in. By exploring these aspects of her home I gained an idea of the sensory embodied experience of Maureen's housework and a way to begin to imagine how these different sensory elements would unite with the physical work she described to produce the emotions of feeling 'soothed' by the ballads, or 'satisfied' by the final result.

Maureen was happy to take responsibility for her housework with some help from her husband with heavier tasks as she required. They lived out what might be termed as a traditional gender role segregated lifestyle in which Maureen maintained her housewifely identity through her everyday embodied actions and performative ascriptions to certain moral values about cleanliness and order that were manifested in her creation and maintenance of a particular sensory home environment.

When I interviewed Malcolm he was a filmmaker, living in a shared rented flat. I had never visited this, the most recent of his homes, before. At the time he was thirty-three, I had known him for almost thirty years, since we met at playschool in Norwich, and had seen many of the numerous homes in which he had lived since we had left our parents' homes to go to university. This flat, Malcolm told me, fitted into the stage he had reached in his life in a particular way. 'I've just moved into this flat so I've recently been trying to make it homely, with sort of next to nothing budget. I moved in here with a trunk of clothes and a rucksack, so it's about trying to get a normal life together.' When he had moved in he had been faced with a sensory challenge:

> [it was] in the middle of February – it was sub-zero, there were no light bulbs in the place. All I could see is this darkness, . . . paper and old socks and piles of rubbish . . . the bathroom had six bin bags in it that they hadn't bothered to throw out and the kitchen had a mouse in it and again, the same amount of bin bags all broken open, so that there was all this kind of smell all around the kitchen.

Five months previously he had resolved this problem by creating a new visual and olfactory order and environment: 'I borrowed a vacuum cleaner. I first picked everything up by hand and sorted everything out. So I dealt with the untidiness first. Sort of, I used bleach and soap and then repainted in the kitchen.' Nevertheless, his approach to his home was quite different from Maureen's. He was determined to combine home-making with a philosophy of 'living well on a non-existent budget'. Like many of my informants he was articulate and reflexive about his own intentionality and the constructedness of his home and he was more explicit than most about the epistemologies that informed his current domestic practices. His choice of objects and textures were contingent on a particular approach:

> I think it's important that . . . [people] . . . see that you can cope without the normal, domestics, material things, but that you don't need to go and buy a £50 table, you can have a sort of disused cotton reel from an electrical shop that you've just found on the street. Cos it actually does the job just as well. I hope I'm the same as this when I make loads and loads of money. I think I will

be because it's just, it's part of me now. So it's kind of an anti-materialist statement of well-being.

As he showed me around his flat, Malcolm told me about the visual
displays he had hung on his wall. First we saw some old sepia prints of
previous generations of his male relatives in military contexts.

> My Grandad, at Gallipoli. That's him on the banks of the Suez Canal. He was
> actually trained in Sheffield, so he's got a connection with this place which I
> wasn't aware of till I got this photograph, but it says Sheffield there. That's
> my Great Uncle Stanley in India . . . Never mind. This guy didn't make it –
> he was killed in 1918. That was my Great Uncle Tom. He was killed in
> November 1918 so he was very unlucky. There's like a family resemblance
> there, which is a bit like myself.

Malcolm told me that he felt this display was about his family history.
However, I felt this masculine military version of history became ironic
as it was set against Malcolm's other visual displays, and the resistance
to the traditional that was part of his everyday life in his flat. Set in
contrast to the other visual narratives in Malcolm's flat, the hegemonic
masculinity and realism represented by these historic photographs was
challenged. In his bedroom he described his understanding of two art
works, emphasizing that what we see is contingent on how and when we
look. The first was a black shape surrounded by an old gilt frame:
'That's my little work of art "old woman collecting wood" we call it. It
could be a sort of devilish friend but if you've got a candle on here, it
lights up the whole wall and looks really nice. It makes this wall look
something different.' The second, a large abstract painting that he
described as follows: 'A friend did that painting for me. She's down-
stairs. And it, the more you look at it, and in different lights, different
things come to the surface. She painted different parts of the painting in
different lights, so some of it's done at night, some of it's done in the
daylight.'

Malcolm's approach to creating his home was also reflected in his
choice of domestic technologies. He had a small and very old electric
vacuum cleaner – 'my wonderful hoover' of which he jokingly told me:
. . . it's super powerful and it's called a Dust Devil. It does this thing
where it kind of stands up . . . so it's almost like a little person.' His choice
of vacuum cleaner, way of speaking about it and treatment of it were
emblematic of his departure from traditional feminine housewifely
approaches to housework. Like many of my informants who pointed out
that they could not 'see' cleanliness in the same way as housewives do he

rejected the feminine housewifely knowledge that informed his mother's approach to cleaning because, in his words:

> *Malcolm:* The flat will never actually be tidy enough for her.
>
> *Sarah:* Or clean enough?
>
> *Malcolm:* Or clean enough. No, it's just, I've got no idea why that is but I suppose, I spent three hours cleaning the kitchen, actually a process of about a week before they came to visit me, and the first thing she did was walk into the kitchen and say, this is filthy. And she then cleaned it for the next three hours and dad and me had to talk to her, sort of while she was in the kitchen. We went out for a two-and-a-half hour walk and when we came back she was still there, re-arranging things. And it didn't really look that much better, to be honest, it sort of, I didn't notice any changes.

When we discussed the notion of a clean home, Malcolm emphasized not only visual but also tactile elements of this, telling me that 'I don't like sort of dog hairs and sticky bits.' In his own home he noted that 'The floor needs doing cos it's kind of gone tacky . . . I don't like tacky floors. I mean that's the point where I clean.' In this interpretation it is not necessarily the visual that signifies that housework should be or has been done, but also olfactory and tactile experiences.

Like everyone I interviewed, Malcolm was engaged in a project of home that was expressive of his biography and identity, using housework practices, visual display, textures, music, smells and creating atmosphere. For Malcolm this involved starting from scratch to make a home on a next-to-nothing budget, combining things he'd found with gifts, cheaply purchased items and his creativity and energy. His home-making project was also part of his project of living well which involved eating healthy food and creating a comfortable environment. He identified this as a recent turning point linked with his decision to do principally paid work rather than working in return for learning new skills. Thus his home was simultaneously emergent from and generative of a wider pursuit and philosophy on life. Partly this meant a break from what he sees as the materialist values of consumption. But the negotiations one enters into with one's home environment are also productive of gender, and Malcolm's home creativity represented a departure from the traditional masculinity of gender role segregation as well as from the traditional feminine housewife knowledge that is associated with the activities he must engage in as a man who does housework. In the following chapters I explore the diverse forms such departures might take as men and women who are not housewives negotiate their relationships with their material and sensory homes. I am not concerned with finding out the 'truth' about their lives at home, but with the ways that they feel they can be 'true' to themselves through the everyday sensory practices and representations that are part of these lives.

–1–

Introduction:
Changing Gender in the Sensory Home

In his introduction to *The Taste of Ethnographic Things* (one of the first anthropological books to broach the question of the senses), Paul Stoller describes how over years of return fieldwork visits to the Songhay people in Niger he realized 'that taste, smell and hearing are often more important for the Songhay than sight, the privileged sense of the west'. In Songhay, he tells us, 'one can taste kinship, smell witches, and hear the ancestors' (Stoller 1989: 5). In this book I suggest that one doesn't need to leave modern western culture to appreciate the importance of senses other than sight Although sight might be privileged by modern western discourse, it is not necessarily the primary sense we engage to understand and create our everyday lives at home. Indeed, in the modern western home, one might feel dirt, smell the landlord's neglect and hear the sounds of being at home. All of these sensory experiences are as real to modern western house dwellers as those associated with kinship, witches and the ancestors are to the Songhay. Such sensory experience, knowledge and practice are a fundamental to the articulation of traditional and contesting gender identities in the home.

In the prologue to this book I have shown how two of my informants, a retired housewife and a single man, spoke of themselves and their homes. Both used metaphors of touch, smell, sound and vision to represent their sensory embodied experiences, knowledge and practices of home. In doing so, they were speaking not simply about what it feels like to clean and decorate one's home but were telling identity stories about themselves – moral tales that could serve to creatively challenge or sustain what they saw as a housewifely approach to the home. In this book I unpack this relationship between individuals' representations of their sensory embodied relationships with their homes and how they situate themselves as men and women in relation to the housewife. I do this through an analysis of my informants' descriptions and demonstrations of their everyday housework and home creativity. By comparing the forms departures from notions of housewifely practice take in two different cultural contexts – England and

Spain – I shall explain how these individual practices can be situated in wider processes of changing gender as it occurs in specific cultural contexts.

Existing anthropological studies of the home, gender and the senses have provided a rich background of insights that inform this study. It is well established that people express (Gullestad 1993: 146–7) or objectify (e.g. Miller 2001a, Clarke 2001) their self-identities through visual/visible and material/tangible practices of home decoration. Such human agency is, however, constrained by the material agency of the home (Birdwell-Pheasant and Lawrence-Zúñiga 1999: 8, Miller 2001a). This has figured strongly in recent work (see Miller 2001a and 2001b) which has showed how homes and the objects in them can impose on the way individual creativity is realized in a particular material space. In existing anthropological literature about the home and its material culture, sensory experience has usually been related to memory and emotion (e.g. Rapport and Dawson 1998a, Hecht 2001, Petridou 2001), clearly important elements of the ways individuals consciously create their homes and experiences of them. Yet existing anthropological studies of the home have not engaged fully with the anthropology of the senses to examine how our everyday relationships with our homes are bound up with sensory perception and metaphor. Neither have theories of embodiment, gender performativity and agency accounted for a sensory – as much as material or architectural – context. I shall explore gender performativity and the home with a specific question in mind: how do people's experiences and understandings of, engagements with and metaphoric references to the aural, tactile, olfactory and visual elements of their homes figure in the way they performatively negotiate their gendered identities in this space? Individuals' gendered performances of housework and forms of home creativity such as hanging a painting, burning oils or candles, or choosing wooden over carpeted floors can be seen as the embodied actions through which they engage with the sensory environments of their homes. Drawing from anthropological uses of Butler's theory of gender performativity, I will explore how the expressivity of everyday gender and the human agency it implies engage with the material agency of the home as formulated by Miller (2001a and 2001b) and Birdwell-Pheasant and Lawrence-Zúñiga (1999). I shall furthermore suggest that everyday practice should be seen not only as engagement with the visual/visible, material/tangible and social aspects of home, but as being integrally related to sensory perception, experience and action. By taking this view, we can see how gender is produced along with the material and sensory environments of home.

In this endeavour I shall both draw from and add to the existing anthropology of the senses. A sensory anthropology as it was promoted in the early 1990s mainly in the work of Classen (1993) and Howes formulated a 'new sub-field' of anthropology of the senses based on the idea that 'it is through a combination of the five senses that human beings perceive the world', but different individuals or societies might combine the senses in different ways, and thus experience reality differentially (Howes 1991: 167–8). However, for Howes 'individual differences in sensory mixes' were not of interest, because 'differences amongst individuals . . . only take on meaning against the background of the culture to which they belong and thus the anthropology of the senses is a sub-discipline concerned with the classification of how "*whole* societies" [original italics] might be more "tasteful" or more orally or visually orientated than others' (1991: 168). This sensory anthropology was a comparative project, concerned with the meanings and importance of different senses to people in other cultures, and comparing these with our (in this case modern western anthropologists') own cultural uses of the senses (Howes 1991: 168–9). Ingold has criticized this comparative approach for its 'mistaken belief that differences between cultures in the ways people perceive the world around them may be attributed to the relative balance in each, of a certain sense over others' (2000: 281). More generally, recent work has defined experience anthropologically as multi- or pluri-sensory. This implies that although different people and different cultures might refer to particular senses when describing specific experiences, their perception of a given experience is not entirely limited to a particular sense. Thus anthropologists should not assume that each sensory metaphor refers to a particular isolated instance of a single category of sensory perception. Rather single sensory metaphors are used as a means of using one sensory category to express perception that is based on pluri-sensory experience. Ingold argues that an anthropology of the senses should attend to the 'creative interweaving of experience and discourses, and to the ways in which the resulting discursive constructions in turn affect people's perceptions of the world around them' (2000: 285). One might expect to find diversity in how sensory metaphors are employed and practices are shaped both within and between cultures. My comparative focus is therefore on how creative individuals in Spain and England involve sensory understanding, experience, metaphor and action in the everyday practices through which they transgress or maintain particular cultural models of gender, cleanliness and homemaking.

There are indeed cultural, as well as individual, differences between the ways housework and decorative forms of sensory home creativity become entangled in Spanish and English people's everyday practices. As my informant Pilar remarked from her own experience: 'The thing is, levels of cleanliness in England and Spain are very different. For example, what I said about having things tidy – in England, in all the houses I've been in, they don't care about that, but I do.' This is also reflected in the way such practices are gendered, not least because in each country gender relations have developed differently. Nevertheless the sensory homes and gendered identities and practices that are the focus of this study are not necessarily directly comparable across Spanish and English cultures. Rather they must be understood in the context of differences between the gender discourses, moralities and physical environments of everyday life in each culture. Existing work has demonstrated the problems of attempting to compare 'whole' societies or cultures. As Strathern insists: 'Instead of dismantling holistic systems through inappropriate analytical categories . . . we should strive for a holistic apprehension of the manner in which our subjects dismantle their own constructs' (1992: 76). Rather than comparing 'systems', cross-cultural comparison might more appropriately involve examining how informants construct and reflect on *their* understandings of the worlds they live in. Moreover, it is necessary to seek out *appropriate* categories for anthropological comparison. Gender has been singled out as a useful category for such comparison. Moore suggests gender is a 'concept metaphor' that might both facilitate comparison and reveal diversity and continuities across space, time and experience. She views 'concept metaphors' such as gender as 'partial' and arguesthat 'their work is both to allow comparison and to open up space in which their meanings – in daily practice, in local discourse and in academic theorizing – can be interrogated' (Moore 1999b: 16). Goddard argues for the comparative potential of gender through a focus 'on the negotiation between the gendered self and the changing character of society' (2000: 4). This facilitates a comparative study of change, allowing analysis of 'the various and often contradictory ways in which men and women, young and old, understand, appropriate and/or reject elements available in global space – frequently identified as "traditional" or "modern" – in their pursuit of individual or collective identities' (Goddard 2000: 5). Following these developments I will explore how Spanish and English men and women situate themselves as gendered individuals (through their everyday actions and verbal descriptions) in relation to what they see as new, old, moral, and personal approaches to housework and home decoration. The point of comparison is a specific focus on how these gendered identities are articulated in the material, sensory and social contexts of English and Spanish homes. However, it would be a mistake to assume that English and Spanish homes are directly comparable. Recent comparative ethnography of the home in Europe has indicated that domestic practices and spaces have different social meanings in different cultural contexts. Comparing

French and English homes and gardens, Chevalier situates her French and English informants' different practices and approaches to home decoration, and their 'passions' of cooking and gardening within specific cultural and historical relationships to land, inheritance and 'nature', showing how in England 'gardening can be considered as an appropriation of nature through everyday practices in the constitution of the domestic sphere' whereas 'In France the area of transformation is not the land but takes place in the kitchen through cooking' (1998: 67). Chevalier's work indicates how different practices and relationships to the material and 'natural' components of 'home' are embedded in specific sets of values and beliefs and long-term historical processes. These values and beliefs in turn inform different uses of space and 'things' in the home and how spaces and objects are implicated in social and kin relationships (in Chevalier's study through inheritance). By comparing different practices, Chevalier shows how cultural differences might be understood without taking recourse to monolithic definitions of cultures. Indeed a direct comparison of the French and English garden would be mistaken because Chevalier's discussion of transformation through the 'passions' of cooking and gardening shows that it is more appropriate to compare the French kitchen with the British garden (see Miller 1998b: 9). Likewise Spanish and English homes and the practices that occur in them are not necessarily directly comparable.

By comparing how gender identities are constituted in the sensory home in Spain and England I aim to develop insights into how different men and women depart from traditional gender roles in different cultures. Statistical studies suggest that gender is changing in what is represented as a similar direction but at different rates in Spain and England. My study suggests that such changes might be occurring in quite different ways that are informed by different cultural and personal knowledge and intentionalities. Statements that claim that 'across Europe women are doing less housework, whilst men are doing more' cannot be taken to mean that across Europe the same changes are taking place everywhere and therefore we are becoming more similar. As Moore has pointed out, 'there is general agreement that globalisation has not produced cultural homogenisation, but is creating new cultural configurations through which people are living out new subjectivities and social relations' (1999a: 11). European homes are key domains in which globalisation or global forces might be experienced. Morley suggests it is at home that people feel the impact of globalization, through their consumption of televised (and on-line) mediated images of 'generic forms' of distant places (2000: 14–15). However, this does not mean that life and experience at home, or homes themselves in different cultural and individual contexts are becoming more alike. Indeed the sensory metaphors and cultural narratives my informants used to describe their relationships to their homes, and the way they interpreted and negotiated with the multiple agencies that intervened in the production of their homes, need to be interpreted as personal affirmations of, or departures from, traditional gender. These might resist or conform to identifiable conventions but are both based on and productive of culturally specific knowledge, values and moralities and take place in culturally specific architectural and design conventions. In the following two sections I provide some background on changing gender and the home by outlining first a wider sociological analysis of change and then the closer context of homes themselves.

Changing Gender in Britain and Spain: The Wider Context

That gender roles and practices are changing across Europe is certain and reflected in existing qualitative and quantitative work in a range of disciplines. Statistical studies of demographics and time use in Spain and Britain suggest that some significant processes of change occurred throughout the 1990s and predict these will continue into the twenty-first century. These studies show how the gendered organization of home life is changing. For instance, Spanish time-use studies suggest men's involvement in domestic work is shifting in a 'really spectacular' way (Miel 1997: 71). In the 1990s men did more housework 'together' with their partners as well as making their own contributions (Miel 1997: 91). Nationally men are taking more responsibility for domestic work, women are doing less housework, and in total less time is dedicated to housework. Statistics from the Instituto de la Mujer show between 1993 and 1996 the amount of housework done by women decreased by 22 minutes to 4 hours 24 minutes a day, whilst housework done by men increased by 9 minutes to 37 minutes and the total amount of housework done decreased by 8 minutes to 2 hours 34 minutes. The organization of housework varies between households and according to other factors such as social class. For example Finkel (1997) found that among lower-class men and women living in nuclear families women carried the main burden of and responsibility for domestic work whether or not they worked outside the home. Men tended to participate more with childcare, occasional tasks, cleaning shoes, taking out the rubbish and paying the bills (Finkel 1997: 12). There is actually significant diversity in how housework in organized amongst Spanish households. In many households the way men participate represents identifiable continuities with existing models of gender role segregation. However, in an increasing number of cases, men undertake traditionally feminine activities. These shifts are also associated with changes in women's lifestyles in the 1990s, with a decreasing birth rate and increasing participation of women in education, training and the labour market. According to a survey carried out in 1996, work was the most important aspect of the lives of 42 per cent of the women interviewed – a marked change from the Franco period; in 1997, 37 per cent of Spanish women were active in comparison with 18 per cent in 1970. Nevertheless, with the exception of public employment, women's work tends to be irregular (Alborch 1999: 138 and see Pink 1997b) and interspersed with periods of unemployment. In general women work shorter hours and receive lower salaries than men. However, Spanish women's aspirations and priorities are changing and in this context of instability many women I met felt pressed to prioritize study and training while working in low-paid insecure jobs on short-term contracts. Such women may not be prepared to prioritize housework and homemaking above career development. Men experience similar problems, and although they are statistically more likely to be in full-time permanent employment, many men work sporadically or are long-term unemployed. For contemporary couples this can impact on how housework is organized. In the existing literature this is often taken to mean the woman works the 'double shift' of taking full responsibility for the home while working full time. Nevertheless it can also mean housework duties are negotiated according to each partner's available time. Moreover with the increasing number of men and women who live alone it is often the case that men and women autonomously organize their own domestic practices, rather than doing so in relation to the contribution of a partner.

Statistical analyses of the changing domestic division of labour in Britain indicate similar shifts. 'Notwithstanding the fact that in 1997 women still performed the bulk of domestic work . . . in relation to changes in time use in other areas of life, the increase in men's participation in domestic work (at least as measured in terms of time contributed) should be regarded as significant' (Sullivan 2000: 437). Sullivan uses her analysis of UK time use diary data to argue that some 'change *is* occurring'. She argues that despite this change seeming negligible when one thinks in terms of men's contributions to domestic work increasing at a rate of less that one minute per year over a twenty-two-year period, the significance of the change is reflected in the '*consistency* of the trend towards men's greater participation in domestic work, and women's decreasing participation in routine housework' (Sullivan 2000: 453). The key trends Sullivan identifies within this are 'a clear reduction in gender inequality in the performance of some of the normatively feminine-associated tasks', 'a larger proportional increase in the time contributed by men from lower socio-economic strata, to a position of near equality with those from higher socio-economic strata' and 'substantial increase in more "egalitarian" couples, especially among the full-time employed' (2000: 453).

The consensus for these studies is that both Spain and Britain are moving slowly towards gender equality. They imply change and diversity by breaking down domestic gender roles by social class, suggesting that some couples achieve equality whilst others are at various distances from achieving it, and that in many households traditional gender role segregation is firmly in place. Nevertheless they cannot document how these changes might be experienced or perceived by the people they concern, identify the intentionalities or agency behind them or account for the specific cultural resources of knowledge that inform everyday practices. Through an ethnographic study of how changing gender is constituted through individuals' everyday relationships with their sensory homes this book locates these changes at the point at which human agents perform gender. It reveals the diversity and unevenness of change as diverse men and women practise their housework and home decoration as modes of resistance or conformity to conventional and contradictory discourses on gender and morality.

Setting the Scene: At Home in England and Spain

If we see changing gender not simply as an outcome of the everyday actions of expressive individuals, but as a result of their negotiations with their material and sensory environments (in this case their homes), then it is essential to account for the ways in which these environments vary. It would be impossible to characterize *the* Spanish or English home per se. However, it is necessary to describe somehow the contexts in which I did my fieldwork. Here drawing from recurrent themes from my interviews and wider experience of homes in these countries I describe similarities and differences between Spanish and English home conventions, textures, smells, sounds and sights. Although my informants did not quantitatively represent contemporary housing trends, in Spain and England I was careful to interview people with different homes, including country houses, city houses and apartments, old and new housing, and rented and owner-occupied homes. Seventeen of the twenty Spanish informants lived in flats and three in houses, while nine of the English informants lived in flats and twenty-one in houses. Below is a description of Spanish homes, followed by a comparative discussion of my English informants' homes.

In my experience most Spanish homes are decorated and furnished to follow conventional architectural layouts, but these might also be resisted and critiqued to varying degrees through altered arrangements. The people who participated in my project, like most Spanish people today, largely lived in modern homes (with the exception of two who lived in renovated country houses) rather than traditional housing (see Sanders 1998 for a review of this). My informants generally lived in flats in two types of building. Courtyard or *patio* buildings back and side onto adjacent buildings leaving only the frontage for external window and balcony space while internal windows face into *patios*. Other buildings allow external windows and balconies at the front and back or along two or more sides. Flat dwellers usually have access to the *terraza* or flat roof, used for drying laundry and providing storage. Some flats have wardens, communal spaces and swimming pools. Living in a Spanish flat involves participating in the *comunidad*, which means contributing fees towards expenses residents jointly incur, and making financial or practical contributions to cleaning and maintaining communal areas. As an English person living in Spain for the first time, I noticed the daily cleaning of shared stairwells, which not only produced a visual result but left the clean smell of bleach lingering in the air as froth and water expelled from the building trickled into the street. Although such activities do not necessarily mean neighbours interact regularly, sometimes collaboration engendered by communal practices leads to close relationships. In general, however, flat dwelling is characterized in the existing literature as being a potentially isolating experience for housewives and flats have been compared negatively to more communal traditional forms of accommodation such as the Andalusian *casas de vecinos* and *corrales* in which neighbours shared a large *patio* which served as a space for cooking, childcare and socializing (see Carloni 1992, Sanders 1998).

Behind the front door of traditional modern Spanish flats is usually an artificially lit entrance area with a mirror and a table decorated with ornaments or flowers. The entrance area leads to a windowless internal corridor, usually long and thin, running the length of the flat with doors leading to bedroom(s), bathroom(s), kitchen and living room. Spanish homes have either tiled or wooden floors, although in the winter rugs are often used in bedrooms and living areas. In Andalusia informants noted the hot climate and the requirement of a cool floor underfoot in the summer mean that floors are tiled and swept and washed with detergent. English and Spanish homes felt very different to me. I walked on different flooring. I smelt different foods cooking as well as the lingering odours of different cleaning products. I felt on my skin and inhaled air of different temperatures and humidity. Spanish living and dining areas are often combined, the latter sometimes in an alcove. A sofa and armchairs usually surround a coffee table, with a television, normally watched at meal times, in view of the dining table. Most of my informants displayed family photographs, heirlooms, books, pictures and ornaments that 'meant something' to them in the living room and sometimes in the entrance. The living room might also have large external windows. Informants with large balconies or *terrazas* emphasized how they enjoyed those areas of their home.

My Spanish informants' bedrooms on the whole tended to be personalized in ways very similar to English informants' bedrooms, usually containing ornaments and/or paintings, and books. In some cases, bedrooms were also used for study (e.g. by students or teachers). Bedrooms might or might not have external windows; in *patio* style blocks of flats they tended to face inwards to the *patio*, leaving the living areas as the only spaces with larger windows and/or balconies. In other flats and houses, bedrooms might have balconies and large windows. In comparison with England, Spanish bathrooms appeared 'clinical', non-personalized spaces. They were tiled, never carpeted and always with a shower and bidet. Most homes with more than two bedrooms had two bathrooms, usually similar in style and layout.

In some larger and newer Spanish flats and houses, kitchens are spacious and incorporate a dining area (called the *office* in contemporary Spanish interior decoration magazines), making the kitchen a family area with a television for mealtimes. However, most informants' kitchens were small, at the back of the flat, or with internal windows facing into the *patio*. Some informants chatted with friends in the kitchen, and those with larger kitchens sometimes ate there when alone. Nonetheless, kitchens were largely functional areas for cooking and cleaning. Spanish kitchens are usually tiled from floor to ceiling and never carpeted. They are fitted with cupboards and appliances and, in contrast to English kitchens, contain dish-drying racks, where crockery is stored, in a cupboard over the sink. My Spanish informants did not personalize their kitchens with ornaments and pictures but kept clear surfaces and walls. Their kitchens were nevertheless personal, expressive areas and they put significant thought into designing or planning new kitchens. Even those who had no scope to change their kitchens had functional objects that 'meant something' to them. In one building of six flats, neighbours communicated through their kitchen windows that opened into the same common *patio* space. This was almost exclusively a feminine practice engaged in by women who saw themselves as housewives, although the men sometimes also participated. Neighbours also collaborated by sharing washing lines that stretched across the *patios* and were accessible only through opposite bedroom windows. However, such living arrangements are neither always possible nor to everyone's taste. Many people do not wish to live in close proximity to their neighbours; they do not want internal windows through which they might glimpse or be watched by their neighbours, hear their talk or television or be subjected to the strong cooking smells of their grilled sardines. In this context, privacy itself is conceptualized as a sensory experience.

The entrance areas to English homes, which often have two rather than one entrance, struck me as quite different to Spanish entrance areas, and there seems to be more variation in how English people create their entrances. For English informants living in the countryside, the back door was usually the functional entrance, to prevent dirt from outdoors being taken into the front, carpeted part of the home. In both country and city houses the 'porch' or entrance area was used to hang coats, and store shoes that would be changed as people went in and out. Entrance areas in England were less decorative than those in Spain. Rather than places to display ornaments, they were spaces for transition between outdoors and indoors. The entrance would generally lead on to a hallway, although in some terraced houses one entered the living room immediately. Hallways tended to be decorated with photographs, paintings and sometimes ornaments.

In living rooms there were familiar themes; as Chevalier (1995: 30–1) has noted, living rooms in England usually contain a three-piece suite, dining room table and chairs, coffee table, television and/or fireplace (one of which is the room's focus). In contrast to Spain, where the television was the focal point in direct view of the dining table, in England the television was the focal point for the three-piece suite (although sometimes this conventional layout might be ironically parodied). Living and dining rooms (often combined) were areas for displaying paintings, family photographs, ornaments and things that 'mean something'. Whereas in Spain walls were usually whitewashed, in England walls were often decorated with brighter and darker colours, or wallpaper. Living room floors were wooden or, more usually, carpeted, but never tiled. English informants, concerned that their homes smelt 'right', used scented candles and oils in living areas.

The sizes of kitchens varied from tiny walk-in spaces to big country kitchens. Strikingly different from Spanish kitchens, even the tiniest English kitchens are rooms to be 'lived in' and were personalized with displays of ornaments, photographs and drawings. For instance, Christine's kitchen housed her collection of ornamental ducks and Jenny's was decorated with pictures drawn by her friends' children. Malcolm had 'invented' elements of his kitchen, and Ben's tiny and 'inconvenient' kitchen was decorated with personal photographs and functional souvenirs. Whereas food tends to be concealed in Spain (often due to the heat), English informants used food and drink as expressive objects. Simon, who is half Thai and had recently been to Thailand to meet his relatives for the first time, had a box of Thai beer on his kitchen surface, whilst Ben's grill boasted a set of foreign coffees. English informants also used their kitchens as 'admin' areas, allocating spaces such as a kitchen surface alongside the window, fitted kitchen shelves or wall areas to give 'admin' a visible presence. For example, as I interviewed one informant, a letter offering him a council flat arrived. This significant change in his domestic life was placed against the wall on his kitchen table.

English bathrooms similarly differed from their Spanish counterparts. Sandra who had recently moved into her council house described her project to create a 'homely' but 'different' bathroom: 'Everybody has a dolphin in their bathroom, everybody has fish, mermaids, ships. I'd like to get away from that . . . I'd like to do something completely wrong for a bathroom, you know . . . I'd want it so it looked nice but mainly no fish, nothing like that.' Jenny, who also lived alone, displayed a number of objects in her bathroom, including a mask from the Beijing Opera, and an empty box, which depicted a historical theme. However, these items were not exclusive to her bathroom, but were equally acceptable in other rooms, as she explained 'this will be part of my moving round of objects' and the mask 'used to be in my bedroom so I moved that. And my mobile' it was probably moved 'I think because I put the box above my bed'. English and Spanish informants, especially women, also used their bathrooms differently. In contrast to Spanish informants, for whom the bathroom was a functional space for washing themselves, putting on make-up and drying their hair, some English informants liked to relax in the bath with candles and a glass of wine, but, with no power points in the bathroom, styled their hair in their bedrooms.

These differently organized material and sensory homes formed the setting for my fieldwork and the physical environments in which my informants lived out their gendered identities.

Background to the Research

The research for this project was carried out between 1999 and 2000 as part of two video ethnography projects funded by Unilever Consumer Science. This book is based mainly on the first, *Cleaning, Homes and Lifestyles*, initially developed with Katie Deverell at Unilever Research. In this project I interviewed twenty men and women of different ages in Spain (in Andalusia, Valencia and Madrid provinces) and twenty in England (in the Midlands, East Anglia and London). At the time I was thirty-three, and based at the University of Derby. I used a snowball method of recruiting informants, working along networks of people I had already interviewed. The sample was based on an analysis of the changing statistical profile of Spanish and British households, and intentionally gave only a small space to the housewife and nuclear family which have been the focus of most existing sociological studies of the domestic division of labour and the family. Instead I focused on the diversity of contemporary masculinities and femininities as they are articulated in the home, encompassing different generations, occupations, sexualities, people living alone, in couples and in families and of different social and economic classes. During fieldwork I stayed in the houses of some informants, giving me a chance to participate in their everyday lives in their homes and experience the sensory environments they lived in. This work was also informed by my existing knowledge about some of my informants, my experiences of living in a number of Spanish and English homes over the previous years and my fieldwork in Spain since 1992. This material is supplemented by a second study carried out in 2000 (in collaboration with Jean Rimmer of Unilever Research and Marie Corbin of the University of Kent) again focusing on domestic identities and lifestyles but this time especially concerned with laundry in the home. For this project a professional market research recruiter found our informants, providing twenty people, mostly part-time housewives with children. This study, which was completed once I was working at Loughborough University in 2000, gave me insights into the worlds of housewives that helped me to understand how other contemporary men and women depart from what they regard as traditional masculinity and femininity as invested in the housewife and her husband.[1] The case studies presented in this book draw from selected interviews from each of these projects.

Originating as it has from an applied anthropology project, however, this project raises some broader issues. Some would question the status of this work as 'real' ethnography. Certainly it did not involve long-term participant observation of a Malinowskian kind. This question is not simply specific to this project but invokes the wider question of the relationship between 'pure' and applied anthropology and the validity of defining anthropology by its method in the twenty-first century. There are two arguments that question the continued value of an insistence on conventional long-term participant observation. The first, already developed in the context of academic anthropology, comes from those who suggest that we need to adapt old anthropological methods to suit new research contexts. This is outlined in Chapter 2 in a discussion of the nature of fieldwork in and about the home. The second, coming from practitioners of applied anthropology, argues for the value of different methodologies (that might involve shorter-term fieldwork) that are nevertheless anthropologically informed. Because for reasons of time, ownership of data and informant and commercial confidentiality applied projects are often not published as academic texts this issue has not been satisfactorily addressed in existing work. Contrasted with purely academic research, applied anthropological research often involves researchers working to shorter and tighter timescales, earning higher salaries, having access to bigger project budgets and producing reports that are accessible to busy professionals and informed by, but unfettered with, theory (see Pink forthcoming). Nevertheless behind the scenes of these visible work processes are usually professionals who have been trained as PhD anthropologists and retained their anthropological identities and approaches. Their research projects are anthropologically informed from design to completion; they use their anthropology not only to undertake their research, but also to understand and thus communicate in the organizational cultures they work in. Their argument is that we should not essentialize social anthropology by defining it in terms of its method, but that a more open approach that defines anthropology as a way of understanding the world is more appropriate. An implicit aim of this book is to present a project that began its life as applied research as a valid anthropological investigation that was from the outset simultaneously informed by theoretical and methodological principles of social and visual anthropology.

The Book

This book attempts to draw together three key themes: the sensory and material home; the gendered agency of men and women; and cultural specificity. It conceptualizes the home as a sensory and material domain and explores it as both a context and outcome of changing gender.

In the following chapters the same theoretical concerns underlie my methodological and substantive discussions as I examine the relationship between sensory experience, metaphor and representation. Therefore these questions are first set out in Chapter 2 where I reflexively discuss a series of issues raised by doing fieldwork in the sensory home. In Chapter 3 I investigate how gender is constituted in the home by examining the insights that can be developed by combining two areas of the existing anthropological literature: gender, performativity and practice; and the approaches of material culture studies to the home. I suggest that a model of gender performativity that emphasizes human agency and creativity can reveal how continuity and change are articulated through individuals' everyday practices in their homes. Chapter 4 develops this by incorporating further insights from the anthropology of the senses to outline the notion of the sensory home. I argue that the performativity discussed in Chapter 3 is realized through sets of sensory practices and represented through sensory metaphor. It is through their sensory engagements with their environments that creative individuals contest, resist and depart from conventional or normative housewifely gender identities. Having established this theoretical understanding of gender and home in chapters 3 and 4, in the following three chapters I discuss how changing gender is constituted in talk and performance in the video and tape-recorded interviews and by implication in everyday life. In Chapter 5 I focus on how change might be perceived, by exploring my informants' understandings of traditional gender, through a focus on the housewife. Then in chapters 6 and 7 I discuss how my non-housewife informants departed from the everyday sensory knowledge and practices associated with housewifely femininity. To conclude, in Chapter 8 I draw these findings together to reflect on their implications for an anthropological approach to sensory experience, practice and change.

Finally, a note about what this book does *not* cover. This is partly to waylay potential criticisms of my approach to the more negative aspects of the situation of women and gendered power in Europe. The home is not always a site for the production of happy empowered identities, but might also be a place of violence, uncomfortable secrets and suffering. My interviews focused on very different aspects of home life and this work has not incorporated the physical and mental domestic cruelty, violence and abuse that form part of the everyday home lives of many women and men in Spain and England. That would be another project.

Notes

1. Elizabeth Shove has also analysed my interviews from this project in Chapter 8 of her sociological book *Comfort, Cleanliness and Convenience* (2003). She asks how conventional laundry practices are transformed. This means at one level looking at what 'collective specifications of service' (normative values about how laundry should be done) have to do with the way multiple adaptations of textiles, detergents and washing machines are integrated. At another level it means examining how what people describe as 'their way' of doing the laundry is constructed (Shove 2003: 166). The sample of informants for this laundry study was likely to produce a relative degree of uniformity and shared values given the socio-economic and cultural class of the informants selected. In criticism of Shove's analysis I

would argue that more attention to non-housewife informants would have indicated more diversity than Shove's analysis of conventional practices suggests. Her work nevertheless offers a useful perspective on wider processes through which domestic practices (such as the shift from boiling to machine washing) and beliefs and values attached to them occur.

2

Video, Performance and Experience: Researching and Representing the Sensory Home

The anthropology of the home and the anthropology of the senses both involve ethnographic methods and contexts that go beyond traditional methods of participant observation. They demand we enter different spaces and attend to different types of experiences and relationships. Carrying out visual ethnographic research in the home raises a set of issues of its own. In this chapter I examine how these intersect through a discussion of three key themes: the sensory home as a context for researching changing gender; the relationship between the audio-visual and the other senses in visual research; and the use of anthropological writing to represent research about sensory embodied experience.

The Home as Research Context

Recent anthropological interest in the home can be linked to both new approaches to anthropology and the changing sociological context in which we do ethnography. The anthropology of the modern western home partly responds to issues raised by the late-twentieth-century crisis of representation, which might be seen 'as a crystallisation of uncertainties about anthropology's subject matter (traditionally 'the other'), its method (traditionally, participant observation) its medium (traditionally, the monograph) and its intention (traditionally that of informing rather than practice)' (James et al 1997: 2). Such studies of modern western individuals in familiar places focus on intimate rather than public spheres of life, and exchange long-term participant observation for interviewing, conversation and new types of collaboration with informants. They involve new configurations of the relationships between anthropologist and informant. When developed as ethnographic film projects they also seek new ways of representing these intimate worlds. Doing anthropology *at* home as well as *in the* home challenges traditional ethnographic fieldwork narratives. Whereas conventionally the field was constructed as specifically *not* home (Amit 1999: 6), fieldwork in the home corresponds with an alternative fieldwork narrative whereby home and field are more closely interwoven through the autobiographical narrative of the fieldworker (see Kulick 1995). When anthropologists do not go to some distant land, collect data and then bring it home, the relationship between the research and the researcher's everyday life becomes all the more significant as alterity and sameness are sought in more familiar contexts. This not only brings about new ways of working but new forms of reflexivity and consciousness for the ethnographer. I have had homes in Spain and England. As I went home between interviews, experienced the sensory environment of my own home and did my own housework, I reflected on how my own experiences and practices mirrored and contrasted with those of my informants.

In addition to having my own comparative domestic practices I shared a wider sociological context with my informants, where I lived, not simply as an anthropologist, but my own everyday life. Many people undoubtedly see themselves as living in territorially based communities (see Moore 1999a: 16, Amit 2002), and some anthropologists argue long-term fieldwork in one locality should be the distinguishing principle of anthropology (e.g. Englund and Leach 2000). Nonetheless approaches that assume culture or social relationships are fixed in one place are not always appropriate. Contemporary research (that is nevertheless informed by theoretical and methodological principles of anthropology) has developed other strategies guided by revised understandings of how and where contemporary lives are lived. Miller identifies the home as a key site for research in the contemporary context in which we live because 'In industrial societies, most of what matters to people is happening behind the closed doors of the private sphere' (2001a: 1), therefore, 'if this is where and how life is lived, it is very hard to see a future for an anthropology that excludes itself from the place where most of what matters in people's lives takes place' (2001a: 3). Of course Miller's point should be taken on the understanding that much that people do in their homes is also mutually embedded with what they do outside their homes. Home life should not be studied in isolation. Nevertheless Miller is correct to suggest that contemporary lifestyles demand a new method that departs from the community study approach. In fact doing ethnography in the home often involves a kind of multi-sited research (Marcus 1995: 51). Fieldwork is spread between different homes and individuals that refer to common cultural conventions and practices but are not necessarily connected. It might also involve further interaction with these individuals outside their homes (although this extension can fall outside the brief of studies of home life). Moreover, as Miller stresses, in modern western society, doing ethnography in the home differs from traditional ethnography in that researchers usually visit, rather than live with, their informants. They may find 'there is no particular community and there is no reason to expect that knowing one family will lead to an acquaintance with their neighbours' (Miller 2001a: 3). Sociological analyses of the way human relationships are changing in contemporary England support these understandings of this fieldwork context. Pahl's study of friendship in England shows how the 'modern focus on friends provides a challenge to conventional, traditional thinking about the family and communities' (2000: 3). He suggests we should see people as individuals who are members of 'personal communities of friendship' rather than work or local communities. My informants likewise spoke of networks of friends, and relatives, often spanning several cities or countries. Some were friends with their neighbours yet their connections to others through family and friendship links were based on networks and activities, rather than locality. This might mean that their most intimate contacts were a bike ride down the road, but they were just as likely to be a drive across the country or even a flight overseas. In England and Spain my fieldwork was multi-sited. My informants were individuals who were not necessarily connected to each other through local community links (although some were friends or related to each other), yet whose different domestic practices and spaces were informed by shared cultural knowledge and discourses.

Representing the Self in the Home

My meeting with each informant in her or his home involved a tape-recorded interview of about an hour, focusing mainly on aspects of gender identity and lifestyle, to develop an overview of each individual's social world and networks outside their home, their aspirations and projects of self and of home long, and their everyday lifes and activities. A video interview, also about an hour, followed: using a small digital video camera with a fold-out screen I asked my informants to show me their homes in the form of a 'tour' of the home. Most of them told me they found the experience interesting and enjoyable. For some our discussions of housework were amusing; housework was distant from their usual expressions of self-identity, and they were given an opportunity to experiment with a new vehicle for narrating this identity.

Using this method I largely relied on what my informants said they did or how they represented what they did visually on video. However, I was usually with each informant for three or four rather than two hours and also socialized outside the home with, and stayed in the homes of, some

informants in both countries. This allowed me to think about their interviews in relation to my experience of their everyday lives as they were
lived, and where the practices they described to me unfolded. This
provided a kind of triangulation that addressed the old anthropological
question of the difference between what people say they do and what they
really do. However, a degree of self-reflexivity and exploration of informants' consciousness was also embedded in the interviews. For example,
we focused on the relationship between how a home ideally should be run
and the ways that this might be deviated from. My informants often
reflected on what 'should' be done, and what in contrast they felt they
really did. For instance, housewife informants discussed with me what a
'good housewife' would do, and reflected on how far they were personally prepared to go towards meeting that ideal. In contrast women who
did not ascribe to a housewife identity described similar housewifely
models and, determined not to meet them, they apologetically admitted
living up to some of their requirements. This does not necessarily close
the gap between what is said and what is really done, but by working with
informants in this way I sought to take seriously their own self-conscious
accounts of their everyday lives at home. Moreover in our video tours I
examined and experienced with them the material and sensory outcomes
of their activities to develop as loyal as possible an account of how their
everyday lives were lived and the knowledge and values they were
attached to. We explored instances of their not meeting what they saw as
the ideal or their own personal ideal, as well as the different verbal and
practical strategies they might use to represent this to others. This
included their descriptions as well as probing about the odd unwashed-up
saucepan or dusty surface we might encounter, and a discussion of how
they might have prepared their home for my visit. In fact most of the
people I interviewed were acutely aware of how, as they moved through
different contexts, they might manipulate the way they represented their
identities to produce explanations for the material state of their homes
that they felt were not really true. For example, Pete described how he
represented himself as 'eccentric' to 'pass off' his untidy home to his
friends.

> I'd love it to appear nice and clean and tidy and, but I know that's not going
> to be like that. It's hopeless trying to expect that. So I tend to make a talking
> point of my eccentricity and the fact that it's a pigsty, you know, wallpaper's
> coming off the walls. And I think they think it's quite amusing really.

Nevertheless Pete told me he found it difficult to stick at housework and
decorating, that he had a low boredom threshold and 'I think secretly I'm

quite lazy. I think I'll work hard. I think I've got a working class guilt thing about relaxing, you know. If I have time off I feel guilty. But secretly I think I could be quite lazy.' For his friends, Pete consciously constructed an 'eccentric' masculine identity that ought to excuse his approach to his home. Nevertheless he claimed that his real reasons for doing little housework were not directly related to this identity. In both their everyday lives and in our interviews, my informants self-consciously and reflexively used gendered categories to represent them-selves, to give meanings to their housework and home creativity practices, and to attach moral judgements to their statements. Working with such skilled negotiators of gender, a reflexive focus on the individ-ual, the specific and particularly on consciousness and self-awareness (mine and informants) was crucial.

Audio-visual Representations in the Home

Doing research in the home means entering private spaces and often asking people about activities that they do not usually speak about. As Miller emphasizes, ethnography in the home is inevitably intrusive (2001a: 1), and involves making decisions about what will and will not be revealed. Indeed, some of my informants did not want their domestic practices and strategies to be revealed to others. Moreover for many of my informants their homes were intricately bound up with transitions in their self-identities and relationships and important life events, some of which had been difficult and painful. It was impossible for them to speak about their lives in their homes without relating them to these experi-ences. Doing research in the home is not just about prying behind closed doors, but about entering the space where people work out issues in their lives privately for themselves. I asked my informants to choose whether or not they would like their interviews to be used in my published work and if they would like their real names to be used. I have not used the interviews of the few I could not trace. Initially I briefed my informants, telling them that they should not feel they had to discuss or show me anything they did not feel comfortable with. Before we started to video I gave them brief instructions regarding what I would like to see and probed about certain objects, practices and areas of the home according to my interview checklist. The 'tour' narrative was nevertheless constructed in terms of how each individual interpreted that activity and simultaneously used the activity as a means of self-representation. Finding her or himself in a unique situation, each individual sought a known narrative through which to interpret the interview and referred (sometimes ironically) to this as they showed me their home. For example, some referenced *Hello* magazine style narratives, either to conform to this style or to joke about the vast difference between the polished homes shown in magazines and their own homes. Some adopted a 'confessional' or self-reflexive stance, turning the tour into a journey of self-knowledge as they pondered over how particular instances of housework or home creativity might be embedded in their own psychologies. Others played with the type of narrative they might follow if showing the house to a prospective buyer. Each individual found a way of managing the interview and video tour in a way she or he felt comfortable with and framed their performance with particular issues and concerns that were prevalent at that point in their lives. I similarly found myself trying to fit as best I could with my informants' agendas, to explore what was important to *them* as well as probing 'underneath' their narratives and posing the questions I wanted to ask.

Inevitably, unequal power relations are implied when the researcher holds the camera and the informant is filmed. I tried to reduce this imbalance by showing most informants the first few minutes of footage to give them an idea of how and what I was filming and how they appeared on film, following what they suggested I film and giving them a final veto over the images of themselves that would be viewed in public or published. Because of the intimacy of our encounters I also often felt scrutinized, when some informants asked me to reciprocate by telling them about myself after the interview, when they passed judgments on me on the basis of our encounter, and by my own spoken presence on the video tape, revealing equally my performance as a researcher. As such '[t]he anthropologist as subject is encompassed within the same frame as the subjects of anthropological enquiry, is coeval with them, and is constituted through relations with them'. This depends on 'a more nuanced recognition of locations, positionings and subjectivities than a previous view of anthropologist/informant relations as simply an interaction of autonomous selves, a relation of us and them separated by cultural difference' (Moore 1999a: 19). However, attention to positionality needs to be balanced with an analysis of the sort of boundaries that we consciously or unconsciously create in our interactions with others. Indeed the interview process itself might inspire informants to self-define as separate from the researcher. As MacDougall puts it. 'the presence of an anthropologist (with or without a camera) can be a significant catalyst in altering people's awareness of themselves' (1998: 27). For example informants (and anthropologists) may use narrative to distinguish between their private and researched/researching selves. As I noted above, my informants did this to varying degrees, selecting existing narratives with which they felt comfortable as reference points in our interviews. In his analysis of 'hard sell' Rapport suggests 'commercial performance is found to be a surface beneath which are persons able, through narrative, to maintain and control sense of self; through the performance of personal narratives (part voiced, part unvoiced) individuals create spaces for themselves beyond the public surfaces of the exchange, affected by it to varying extents but in no measure the effect of it' (1998a: 180). The performance element of our interviews was crucial, and, although my informants didn't use the hard sell narrative Rapport describes, they did adopt narrative as a way of selecting what it would be appropriate to reveal and conceal. In this sense each video interview created a one-off context for performance, a 'stage' for which my informants prepared themselves in a range of different ways.

To analyse the performances meant not simply taking informants' representations at face value, but remaining aware of how people might employ different devices to express their conformity to or rejection of conventional gendered ways of thinking about or doing housework. The way some men used mimesis and irony to speak about, and embodied actions to demonstrate or animate, housework tools is a good if maybe more exaggerated example. In the prologue I described how Malcolm rejected housewifely knowledge and ways of seeing his home. In our interview his mini-hoover became characterized as 'almost like a little person', in a story that I collaborated in as we delighted in Malcolm's demonstration of how the hoover can sit and stand. In his words, 'This is the main cleaning implement and I think it stands up . . . [Switches on vacuum] . . . so it's almost like a little person.' Other men, also sought ways of animating the objects they used for cleaning, of equating housework with play, using 'imaginary' companions embodied in the forms of cleaning tools, and creating a parody of housework through which to describe their actual practices. For example, in Spain, Gonzalo was also in his thirties and lived alone. In his bathroom we discussed his bathroom sink, he pointed out his 'favourite soap dish' and he showed me the sponges he used to clean the sink, animating them as he spoke: 'Hello, little sponge, smile! Look, one's fallen off. This one's for when its more stubborn, this is the normal one and this is for the final touch.' Through these games these men tell self-aware stories of how their everyday practices transgress conventional housewifely methods. These are 'identity stories' in which 'traditional' and 'housewifely' practices and worldviews are transformed, through the representation of realities in which informants' everyday practices are based on other worldviews where cleaning implements become cartoon characters. In contrast other informants praised their vacuum cleaners within different narratives. Maureen set hers in a serious discussion of what she enjoyed about her housework telling me that 'I must admit I quite like the hoover now because of the new one I've just bought – that Dyson. Because it does lift up a lot of the dirt that you didn't think was in the carpet.' In this case Maureen's reference to the Dyson was not only concerned with her aim to maintain a home that was more than visibly clean. It also related to the gendered practices and knowledge she shared with one of her local friends who also had a Dyson and from whom she had sought advice before purchasing it.

Doing such research in the home inevitably means that rather than living the everydayness of people's lives alongside them, the researcher is learning about people's representations of their everyday lives. Video and tape-recording these representations produces a different sort of material to traditional field notes produced as part of a community study. Audiovisual studies are often based on more intense and concentrated interactions in which researcher and informant work together to complete a task. This task is both practical and about ideas and understanding. It might lead the informant (and anthropologist) to arrive at a new level of self-awareness, which in itself will be reflected in the way her or his representations of their everyday life are framed. Such research is not entirely visual and verbal, but also involves the researcher's embodied sensory experience of both informants' home environments and of their representations of the way they create and experience their homes.

Video Research in the Sensory Home

To access embodied sensory knowledge in anthropological fieldwork 'the anthropologist has no choice, but to use body and soul in addition to intellect, as a means of approaching others' experience. Linguistic utterances might provide a clue, but they cannot be depended upon. There is also the full range of bodily senses' (Okely 1994: 61). Interviewing people in their homes about their experience of home exposes researchers to both representations of sensory experiences and to their own sensory experiences. To be able to account for this we need to understand sensory experience on three levels, first through an anthropological theory of the senses, second by interpreting fieldwork as a sensory embodied experience, and third by interpreting how and why informants use sensory metaphors to express their experiences. The question of how anthropologists might understand and represent other people's experience in written ethnography has already been problematized. We know we cannot get into other people's minds (Fernandez 1995: 25) or their bodies. Rather, anthropologists' understandings of informants' words and actions express *our* consciousness, not *theirs* (Cohen and Rapport 1995: 12). Using video to research other people's sensory experience raises additional issues. With video-informants and researchers can use both spoken words and physical actions to represent their sensory experiences. However, because it privileges the visual and the spoken its interpretation needs to be informed by a theory of the relationship between and amongst the visual and the other senses.

The relationship between the senses has always been a concern for anthropologists of the senses. Classen, Howes and Synott (1994: 9) wrote of a 'multi-sensory context', although their main concern was with distinguishing the different sensory mixes that could be found in different cultures. Most notably they argued that modern western culture privileges the visual while other cultures might give more importance to smell or sound, for example. The interconnectedness of the senses has been described by writers drawing from a range of academic traditions who have sought to stress the relationship between touch, vision and consciousness (e.g. Taussig 1991, MacDougall 1998, Stewart 1999: 32). Seremetakis emphasizes the impossibility of separating different sensory experiences, referring to the 'tactility of smells' and how 'each smell generates its own textures and surfaces' in her sensory memories of her childhood in Greece. She describes 'the oregano bunch hanging over the sheep skin containing the year's cheese; the blankets stored in the cabinet which combine rough wool with the humidity of the ocean . . . the fresh bread in the open covered with white cotton towels' (Seremetakis 1994: 218). Ingold similarly argues that to understand sensory experience and perception we should not see the senses as separate modalities, but extends this by drawing from the biological argument that sensory perception is in fact similar for any of the senses. Thus he urges anthropologists to explore the common ground between seeing and hearing (and I would add touch and smell) (2000: 287) rather than seeing them as isolated and opposed. Ingold asserts that modern western philosophy's claim that vision is the hegemonic sense through which knowledge is objectified in modern western society is unfounded. There is, he argues, actually 'nothing natural or pre-ordained about this opposition: as often as it is reasserted in academic books it is belied in our own experience' (2000: 287). It follows from this that what is really of interest is how different people use different sensory metaphors to understand their experiences and practices and represent them to others. I take this question up empirically in Chapter 4.

As the above writers propose, it is problematic to separate the visual from the other senses, whether in terms of a biological perception, cultural theory, ethnographic experience or local epistemologies. Any fieldwork context can be understood as a multi- or pluri-sensory environment where both researcher and informant are constantly experiencing and interpreting sensory stimuli. Within this, people's everyday uses of sensory metaphors and actions might be researched and analysed. My informants and I were seeking ways to express and give meanings to their sensory experiences and practices on video by using verbal and visible embodied metaphors. This meant that single sense metaphors were most frequently used to distinguish, identify and evoke particular sensory experiences and actions that were linked to the identity stories my informants told me. As we have seen in the Prologue, Maureen and Malcolm did not speak of multi- or pluri-sensory experience, but of the smell, sight and feel of their homes. In the tape-recorded interviews we discussed olfactory, tactile, audible and visual aspects of informants' homes. In the video tour we explored some of the visible, and material and experiential manifestations, of (e.g. open windows, perfume and body spray bottles, cleaning products, air fresheners, laundry, the presence of radios and CD players etc). My informants often indicated things that I must 'get on the video', for example the action of opening a 'smelly' cupboard or spraying perfume in the air for me to sample, or showing me where we could hear but not see the squeaks of bats that lived in the eaves. In this context I could record the visual and verbal metaphors they used to express their sensory experiences, but I could not access the actual experiences or processes of perception themselves because in this way the senses are 'mediated, interpreted and conceptualised' (Okely 1994: 47). However, we can reflexively draw from our own experiences. Through being there, we cannot claim to have had precisely the same sensory experiences as others, but we can 'creatively construct correspondences between' experiences (Okely 1994: 47). Nevertheless we can go beyond informants' words and the visual and performative metaphors they use to represent knowledge to us, by using our own 'full range of bodily senses' to empathise with their sensory experiences (Okely 1994: 61).[1]

A strand of work in the anthropology of the senses sets out an agenda for sensory embodied research (e.g. Seremetakis 1994, Okely 1994, Stoller 1989, 1997). Here the production of ethnographic knowledge is regarded as a fundamentally embodied and sensory process. This approach advocates a reflexivity that depends on the ethnographer's self-awareness of the sensory experiences though which he or she comes to understand other people's lives, with examples from rural Greece (Seremetakis 1994), Niger (Stoller 1989, 1997) and France (Okely 1994). Okely's experience in particular demonstrates how in modern western society attention only to what we see and hear might not be enough. Okely describes how she only understood her elderly informants' comparisons of their lives in the municipal institutions they inhabited with their previous lives in their own village homes, though her own sensory experiences of village life. It was only after Okely had 'absorbed something of the conditions of their past existence through living in their former locality and experiencing its tastes, sounds, smells and sights' that she could understand their loss (1994: 58–9). Such sensory experiences and moments of understanding cannot be visually recorded with a video camera. However, the video camera should not be seen as an impediment in the ethnographer's ability to experience them. Ethnographic filmmaker David MacDougall suggests that a similar process is involved when we understand other people's sensory experiences with or without the camera: 'we reach out to others with our senses as a sort of probe (in films through the extension of the camera) and make sense of them through what we contain ourselves. Our knowledge is transposed or displaced, toward them, so that it appears to be *of* them. We are using our bodies and cameras as kindred instruments' (1998: 29). Most important here is to reflexively attend to the role of the camera in the particular fieldwork context (see Pink 2001) as part of that sensory world.

The worlds I entered in my informants' modern western homes were not simply sites for the visual objectification of knowledge. Rather smell, touch and sound were equally referred to in their descriptions and were part of their objectification. However, the technologies and methods I used for this project inevitably privileged vision and language. A question remains: are language and vision appropriate for the production of anthropological knowledge about multi-sensory anthropological field-work contexts or the olfactory and tactile experiences that informants refer to? Visual anthropologists have long used the visual and verbal to represent emotional and corporeal experiences and knowledge. Below I reflect on how this questions has been broached in the existing visual anthropology literature, before suggesting how the question of the relationship between the senses in audio-visual research might be addressed.

Visual Anthropological Approaches to Sensory Experience

Although few have engaged fully with non-visual experience and perception, visual anthropologists have certainly recognized their significance. For example Taylor does not recognize 'any one hierarchy of visual or sensuous knowledge' (1994: xiii) and Grimshaw notes that 'anthropologists have sought to escape the tyranny of a visualist paradigm by redis-covering the full range of human senses' leading to 'the development of sensuous perspectives towards ethnographic understandings' (2001: 6). However, little has been done to explore the wider implications of a sensory anthropology for visual anthropology as a whole. Indeed discussion of the visual and the other senses has been largely limited to claiming the potential of ethnographic documentaries for representing sensory embodied experience (e.g. Ruby 2000, MacDougall 1998, 2000).

David MacDougall's work provides a starting point for considering how video might represent and evoke sensory embodied experiences at different stages of the research process. Taking as a key issue the differential abilities of language and images to communicate anthropological knowledge, MacDougall argues that the visual is particularly suitable for representing sensory and embodied approaches to anthropology. Visual representation, he claims, can offer pathways to the other senses and resolve the difficulties anthropologists face in researching and communicating about 'emotions, time, the body, the senses, gender and individual identity', by providing 'a language metaphorically and experientially close to them'. Because the visual has a 'capacity for metaphor and synaesthesia' he proposes that 'Much that can be "said" about these matters may best be said in the visual media' (MacDougall 1997: 287) as opposed to by the written word because the former can facilitate the 'evocation' demanded by the 1980s and 1990s emphasis on the experiential in anthropology (MacDougall 1997: 288). MacDougall also suggests that in addition to its synaesthetic capacity to evoke sensory experience, the visual offers a second route to sensory experience. Like Ingold and Seremetakis, he stresses the inseparability of the senses, drawing from Sobchack (1992) and Merleau Ponty (1992) to approach the senses 'not simply as separate facilities capable of some form of synaesthetic translation, but as *already* interconnected – in fact as the entire perceptive field of the body' (1998: 50). In particular it is the interconnectedness of seeing and touching that MacDougall suggests underlies the filmic communication of sensory experience. Noting studies of blind people who on recovering their sight are unable to recognize objects visually until they have touched them (MacDougall 1998: 50), he argues that touch and vision 'share an experiential field' since '[e]ach belongs to a more general faculty'. Therefore 'I can touch with my eyes because my experience of surfaces includes both touching and seeing, each deriving qualities from the other' (MacDougall 1998: 51). He insists that 'To describe the role of aesthetics properly (its phenomenological reality) we may need a "language" closer to the multidimensionality of the subject itself – that is a language operating in visual, aural, verbal, temporal and even (through synaesthetic association) tactile domains' (MacDougall 2000: 18). He is suggesting that autiovisual media rather than written words might best represent the sensory and embodied aspects of culture and experience.

MacDougall's contribution is important because he acknowledges the relevance of the relationship between the senses for visual anthropology. Here I want to draw from this to discuss the use of video to produce and represent sensory knowledge as part of the research process. While (as I discuss elsewhere) I doubt that as anthropological representation film can live up to the role MacDougall proposes for it (see Pink forthcoming), I shall argue that as a research method video might achieve what MacDougall claims.

Video Research and the Senses

Video research is not simply about visual data collection and it would therefore be wrong to assume that the objective is to visually record other sensory experiences. Instead producing video research footage involves collaboratively producing audio-visual representations of embodied sensory experiences with ones informants. In the prologue I described how I learnt about Maureen and her sensory home. Knowing that we were using the audio-visual (the camera) and the verbal (our tape-recorded conversation) simultaneously, Maureen told me about her sensory experiences of home and housework using the available resources and technologies. Maureen and my other informants were aware of the limits of video. Sometimes they referred to obstructed or faint sounds or sights when, although they recommended I try, they doubted I could 'get it on the video'. Therefore on the videotapes embodied sensory experiences were represented variously. The visible and audible experiences represented other sensory modalities though synaesthesia, including: visual images of embodied actions (informants enacting processes or touching, smelling or stroking objects and spaces); verbal utterances and descriptions; visual images of objects and processes that are metaphors for and evocative of sensory experiences (e.g. candles, oils, perfumes, spaces and actions); and facial expressions. For me to understand these representations when later viewing the videos would require what MacDougall refers to as sharing 'common referents' with the video maker and subjects, in a process by which 'the viewer "fills" or replenishes the image with his or her own bodily experience, inhabiting the absent body represented on screen' (1998: 53). However, the extent to which we can do this is limited. As I have noted above, even when actually doing the research we cannot get into other people's bodies – we must base our understandings on our own consciousnesses rather than theirs. In response to MacDougall's claim that we can touch by seeing I would ask whether when we do so we feel the same textures as ethnographic film subjects? Even when working with materials I have shot myself, although

I can empathize with my informants to guess at what they felt and knew when they touched the surfaces of their homes, I would not claim that this leads me to knowledge of their actual experience. It would be harder still to achieve this when viewing an ethnographic film of a context that one had never experienced.

When we represent sensory experience on video, whether this involves direct observation of cultural performances as they actually take place, or interview led footage with more overt collaboration, enactments and possibly reconstructions with an informant, we rely on the visual and audible utterances to represent sensory embodied experience. In doing so a hierarchy of the senses is created in which the visual and sound are privileged in the process by which video communicates. In this sense the videotapes might be seen as audio-visual ethnographic materials. To make these materials anthropologically meaningful they should not only be understood in the terms MacDougall outlines (above). Rather, they should also be interpreted according to a theory that on the one hand deconstructs the hierarchy of the senses suggested by the audio-visual media, and that on the other hand interprets the fieldwork context as a pluri-sensory domain. It is only by situating these materials anthropologically using theories of representation and of sensory experience that they might be used to study the sensory home.

Using my own video materials to analyse my informants' relationships with their sensory homes I was not confronted so much with the question of how to edit and represent these experiences to viewers, but with that of how to interpret these existing representations of my fieldwork experiences anthropologically. I *had* been there and to a certain extent the videos along with my more general fieldnotes were evocative of that experience. My reading of the actions, objects, utterances and other representations in the videos and transcripts was guided by a pluri-sensory theoretical perspective, a concern with embodiment, the material, gender performances, narrative, self-consciousness and the individual. This sensory experience would also have been accessible to me through making detailed written fieldnotes. Nevertheless, using video has allowed me to bring to the analysis representations of the non-linguistic aspects of the research encounter through what MacDougall calls 'a process of physical engagement' rather than translation (1998: 266). However, my work has a different brief to the film-making that MacDougall writes about, since my videotapes were not made with the intention of producing an ethnographic film. Rather the video interviews were intended as exploratory and collaborative representation of my informants' relationships with their homes, and not for public view.[2]

The Sensory Home and Anthropological Representation

I have presented this work in a written book for several reasons. First, I wanted to present this research in a way that is directly conversant with existing theoretical and ethnographic literature in the fields of gender studies, the home and the senses. To do so requires anthropological writing. Ethnographic film might bring to our attention knowledge and experience that cannot be communicated linguistically. However, it cannot explicitly engage in detail with these bodies of anthropological theory that have been developed as linguistic discourse on their own terms (see also Pink 2004). Second, there are ethical reasons. The video-tapes were made on the understanding that they would not be shown in public and, as I noted above, most of my informants agreed to let me use their interviews but have chosen to remain anonymous in my written work. Third, writing is not totally inadequate for representing sensory experience (c.f. MacDougall 1998: 262). Stoller's (1997) *Sensuous Scholarship* is an example of how this might be achieved. Moreover, as Taussig has suggested, mimesis of a different kind to that we would assume for video also forms part of ethnographic writing through 'the capacity of the imagination to be lifted through representational media, such as marks on a page, into other worlds' (1993: 16). The prologue to this book is an attempt to use written words to represent how my inform-ants created and experienced their homes while also evoking something of the research experience. Using quotations from our interviews and my own descriptions I have presented an account that explores the relation-ship between Malcolm's and Maureen's individual practices, the sensory and material elements of their homes, their values and gendered identi-ties. I have hinted at an anthropological basis for understanding this by stating that such experience is pluri-sensory. This like most typical anthropological writing is an attempt to mix ethnographic description with anthropological theory.

As Hughes-Freeland has pointed out, visual anthropology runs into problems when it starts to think in terms of images *versus* words (2004). The question is not: would images or words represent this work best? Rather: which combination of images and words is the best way possible to represent *this* particular piece of work under *these* present circum-stances?

Notes

1. Indeed recent research in neuroscience associates smell with empathy suggesting that empathy, or 'feeling another's emotions', is related to smell identification (Spinella 2002: 610). Thus, there is a scientific basis for assuming that attention to sensory experience is an important part of ethnography.
2. Selected clips for a limited number of interviews are being used in experimental hypermedia projects that explore the relationship between visual and written anthropology.

3

Theorizing Changing Gender at Home

A consideration of changing gender in the home requires a theoretical understanding of gender and home. In this chapter I draw from recent developments in this area to develop an approach suited to this endeavour. Critical reconsiderations of women's contemporary and historical agency have challenged the theoretical models of women's subordination and patriarchy that dominated past studies of gender in Spain and England (see MacClancey 1996, Pink 1997a, Silva 2000). Here, following these existing correctives, I discuss how housework and home creativity might be seen as instances of women's and men's agency (rather than of their oppression) and as decisive in the production of continuity and change in contemporary gender. First I argue that individual agency in the home is a key force in producing the changing gender configurations I described in Chapter 1. Second I examine the nature of the home as a context in which such agency is articulated. This chapter concentrates on developing these theoretical perspectives in relation to existing work on gender, agency, creativity, consciousness and the material home. In the following chapter these ideas are integrated with a focus on the sensory home.

Much existing literature treats housework and home decoration separately. The former has been largely the concern of sociologists of housework or of the domestic division of labour along gender lines. The latter has attracted the attention of those concerned with material culture studies and interdisciplinary projects of anthropology and architecture. Here, to shift the emphasis away from the visual aspect of home decoration that prevails in existing literature, I use the term home creativity to encompass the embodied experience and production of sound, smell and texture in the home. Nevertheless housework and home creativity are not absolutely separate sorts of activity; both are performative activities and creative processes that affect visual and other sensory results and individuals may perform each in a specific relationship to the other. There are also some significant differences. Home decoration is often seen as more permanent than housework. Housework is associated with the everyday and repetitive performance of tasks that aim to maintain a result or equilibrium, whereas home decoration creates relatively longer lasting effects and is seen as a series of one-off or extra-ordinary rather than everyday activities. However, both are processes of representation and sometimes intentional and creative strategies of affirmation of or resistance to perceived conventions, norms or discourses. Home creativity, like housework, involves repetitive action. This might occur within a circumscribed period of time, such as for painting and decoration. In other cases it might involve periodic replacement of sensory decorations such as scented candles or the switching on and off of music and radio at decisive moments. Indeed repetition can form part of housework and home creativity activities that initially appear spontaneous and non-routine. As Garvey's discussion of the '"incidental" routine' of her informant's periodic reorganization of furniture demonstrates, this form of 'habitualized spontaneity' can involve both repetition and rupture (2001: 49–55). Housework and home creativity are both processes of the constitution of self that involve embodied performative actions, material objects and sensory experience.

Approaches to Housework and the Constitution of Gender

Although anthropological studies have viewed housework as a necessary aspect of the functioning of domestic spheres, anthropologists have rarely focused on housework as *the* theme of their investigations. The sociology of housework has developed as a mainstream topic, the literature of which is, however, framed by theories of binary gender and patriarchy and is largely based on West and Zimmerman's (1991 [1987]) notion of 'doing gender'. This approach disempowers individuals 'who do gender', denying them agency since practices that resist normative gender roles are futile because 'if we fail to do gender appropriately, we as individuals – not the institutional arrangements [based on sex category] – may be called to account (for our character, motives and predispositions)' (West and Zimmerman 1991: 33). The idea that gender is a product of embodied actions seems quite appropriate, nevertheless there are many ways of doing gender, some of which constitute change. Recent work in anthropology and cultural studies has emphasized the relationship between agency and practice, seeing both rituals and everyday performances as not simply 'replication of a given script' but as 'techniques and technologies of the self/selves' (Hughes-Freeland 1998: 3) that construct realities and constitute gendered identities (see Tulloch 1999: 1–8). Moreover, as anthropological theories of gender have emphasized, gender identities are diverse, heterogeneous and 'negotiated', rather than binary and fixed, and are a fundamental aspect of selfhood (Connell 1995, Cornwall and

Lindisfarne 1994c, Strathern 1993, Kulick and Willson 1995). By speaking of 'multiple masculinities and femininities, multiple ways of being masculine and feminine within the same context' (Moore 1994: 61) that may be constructed 'in counterpoint with one another' (Moore 1994: 60) we open a space for alternative gender representations to challenge hegemonic versions, and for individual agents to act as the instigators of change. As Goddard (2000: 3) has noted, since gender identities are so 'integral to the construction of subjectivity and the placing of individuals in the social world' and thus inform discourses of continuity and change, gender analysis is important for the study of agency and experience. Therefore through their individual housework practices men and women may in fact perform genders that refer to, resist or challenge hegemonic discourses. Their domestic activities constitute embodied representations of multiple (even contradictory or competing) ways of being a man or a woman, rather than the binary gender identities assumed by models of patriarchy. Some men and women may enact different elements of their identities in different ways, or perform alternative versions of their gendered selves in different contexts and interactions. Domestic gender is not simply 'done' in one way, and thus 'reproduced' every time it is repeated. By seeing gender as partial and completed only in interactions with other individuals, objects or spaces we can begin to think of individuals' housework practices as performative actions through which they might self-consciously constitute and re-constitute their gendered identities.

Approaches to Home Creativity and Constitution of Gender

Much of the existing literature on home creativity has focused on home decoration, which it has gendered as a feminine activity concerned almost exclusively with the creation of visual and atmospheric 'homely' aspects of the domestic environment. Thus the practice of home decoration has been viewed as a feminine creation of visual imagery and physical and emotional comfort for the consumption of men in the domestic interior. A review of the existing literature on the bourgeois home in Europe in the nineteenth and twentieth centuries (see Morley 2000) indicates that this represents part of the gender role segregation of western modernity that is set within broader sets of dichotomies. Morley draws from Gupta and Ferguson (1997) to characterize the opposition between local and global as a gendered distinction. '[T]he local is understood to be that which is natural, authentic and original, whilst the global is seen as the realm of the external, artificially imposed or inauthentic'; thus the local, associated with femininity, is 'seen as the natural basis of home and community, into which an implicitly masculine global realm intrudes' (Morley 2000: 59). Set within this argument is the idea that women, effectively by creating and decorating the home and maintaining its moral and physical cleanliness, are simultaneously making and maintaining their own 'proper' (normative) femininity. This approach represents a dominant discourse on gender that has been influential throughout the twentieth century and is still at play today. The model also stands for a theoretical gendering of global/local, public/private and street/home that encourages academic characterizations of the relationships between the different spheres in terms of hierarchical gendered power relations and the subordination of women. These dichotomies provide useful ways of thinking about relations of power, but they need to be balanced by ethnographic studies of the complexities of power relations and the detailed distribution of power within or between these spheres. To study changing gender in the home in particular we need go beyond the gendered and gender dichotomies represented in these theoretical visions of the gendered nature of home. Instead we must explore how contemporary men and women constitute their own gendered identities through practices of home creativity that might transgress, critique and contest the hegemonic gender and binarisms represented such in models and discourses.

Such models also preclude the roles of men in home creativity. For example, Morley describes conflict over the home as a gendered conflict, in the C20 manifested in 'a symbolic battle [which] emerges between the figures of the housewife and the modernist architect' (2000: 61). He notes how in the 1950s in England 'housewives subverted the architects' and town planners' modernist aesthetic with the "cosy clutter" of their curtains and heavy drapes' (Morley 2000: 62). It is not unusual for domestic space to be used for purposes and in ways not intended by its designers (see Miller 2001a, Booth 1999). Most studies that reveal such practices have focused on the roles of women as homemakers and organizers of domestic space, which fits well with a theory of feminine (domestic) resistance to masculine (public) framing. This may well have been closer to the empirical reality of the 1950s that Morley refers to. Nevertheless Gullestad's (1993) study of home decoration in Norway shows that, as working-class women began to earn their own wages, shared projects of home decorations in which couples participated together became the norm. In the cases she describes, a gendered division of labour meant women took more responsibility for design, budgeting and purchasing while men did the heavier and DIY work. As such, traditional gender roles were to some extent maintained. Nevertheless the fact that these men were involved in producing, rather than simply consuming, homeliness is key. As Gullestad points out, studies of gender 'in terms of conflicts and contrasts' often leave men's and women's shared concerns unexamined (1993: 128). Moreover a theory that models gender on conflict cannot account for how contemporary men might be involved in creating and changing their homes (in ways that are not simply normative DIY activities) since such a theory would need to feminize men's home creativity. As such it cannot accommodate the ethnographic reality of a more complex array of different gendered ways of home-making. The greater complexity of how multiple masculinities and femininities might become inscribed in the ways different men and women creatively engage with different architectural forms both structurally and decoratively requires a theory of plural gender that distinguishes between the use of binary models that gender particular types of oppression and resistance and the ways in which everyday resistance is embedded in embodied gendered identities, actions, experiences or roles. In short both men and women perform different sorts of masculinities and femininities in their domestic creativity, which might resist or contest modern architectural structures and ideologies in specific ways. Thus we must rethink how practices of homemaking and home decoration have been gendered. Like housework, home creativity can be understood as an activity through which human agents constitute their diverse gendered identities, and as such participate in changing gender.

Performativity, Consciousness and the Anthropology of Gender

To explain how change occurs anthropologists have suggested that individuals' performativity might be a creative means of resisting existing discourses, a process that constructs realities and constitutes change (e.g. Moore 1994, Schieffelin 1998). Proposing we should study the 'agency and intentionality' and 'creativity and constraint' of both public and everyday performance, Hughes-Freeland (and the contributors to her volume, 1998) and Tulloch (1999) suggest performance is an expressive 'technology of the self' that has transformative potential and is thus integral to understanding 'change'. Recent anthropological discussions of gender have also focused on the notion of performativity as a way of understanding hegemonic genders and resistance to them (Morris 1995, Moore 1999b). In particular Morris has argued for a return to Butler's theory of gender performativity that 'rejects the notion of founding acts and posits gender as the product and process of repetition' (1995: 576), thus seeing gender identity as being constituted through everyday or ritualized repetition.

Anthropologists have largely used the notion of performativity to discuss ritualization, public performances and change. Some have also noted the performative aspects of everyday life. Focusing on housework they suggest even the most mundane activities might be performative. For example Rostas follows Humphries and Laidlaw defining ritualization as the non-intentional and habitual carrying out of an activity (1998: 89). In contrast performativity 'entails action that is not prescribed' and involves 'the employment of consciously formulated strategies' (Rostas 1998: 90). In an endnote Rostas uses washing up as an example of the relationship between ritualization and such everyday performativity:

> this [washing up] is precisely the kind of action that is done ritualistically; it is done frequently, usually in the same way, with attention but not conscious intention, other than that of getting the dishes clean, which has become an embodied, habitual activity. If someone carried out this action rather more dramatically than is strictly necessary for the task, with expansive movements and rather amusingly or angrily, for example, then we might want to classify this as 'performance', and look more closely at the performativity, the non-conventionality of the act, the non-habitual nature of it, even at its creativity. (1998: 102)

Schieffelin, questions Rostas to ask whether 'the furrowed brow and/or the clattering and banging of the dishes in the sink' might necessarily entail 'any expressive intent or even awareness of self-revelatory behaviour', suggesting that it might simply be that the washer up washes up in this way when she or he is involved in a particular emotional narrative of elation or anger. In an endnote he elaborates that

> What the performance of ordinary, mindless washing-up activity expresses is an ongoingness in life, the low profile, apparent performative neutrality of familiar convention which forms the background of any situation. Depending on what is happening in the lives of the participants, it may also constitute an 'escape' from the complexities or the rest of the situation, or an abdication of responsibility in an apparent fulfilment of it. Conversely such activity may represent the numbing of self in a stifled life, or a refuge in familiar activity, or many other things. But such activity is always placed in some context – though perhaps in very low performative profile – in relation to the ongoing situation. (Schieffelin 1998: 205–6)

Schieffelin proposes that 'expressivity (and hence performativity) [is] inherent in any human activity in everyday life' although our expressivity is not entirely under our own control, as it also depends on how activities are interpreted by others (1998: 197). Seeing practices in Bourdieu's terms as forming 'the shape of the unthought behavioural regularities of a cultural world' of Bourdieu's habitus 'Practices can be said to emerge from this ground of habitude in the form of structured or "regulated" improvisations when people deal with the situations in which they are involved in customary practical ways' (Schieffelin 1998: 199). For Schieffelin, 'performance embodies the *expressive dimension of the strategic articulation of practice*', and performativity is thus 'located at the creative, *improvisory* edge of practice in the moment it is carried out' although not always consciously (1998: 199).

In this endnote discussion that runs parallel to their essays on public performances, both Schieffelin and Rostas emphasize in different ways that the mundane activities of everyday life can also be performative. Schieffelin is right to expand Rostas' characterization of the performative aspect of washing up to situate it in relationship to the ongoingness of other emotional narratives of everyday life. However, further contextualization is needed. Each instance of washing up needs to be situated not only in the emotional narratives of everyday life but also in the performative narratives that each individual engages in throughout the series of emotional and practical activities she or he enacts at home. The emphasis on the non-intentionality of washing up, as a mindless yet embodied activity involving 'the numbing of self in a stifled life' or a refuge from the complexities of intentional action, implies housework is not an activity through which the self-conscious agency of performative creativity is likely to be engaged and subsequently suggests change is not instigated from the agency associated with the performativity of housework. Thus the potential of women and men as creative agents in the home is denied and the home is not recognized as a locus of changing gender. The problems of this approach are also emblematic of the limits of Bourdieu's theory of practice from which Schieffelin draws: as Morris points out, in Bourdieu's work 'reiteration' was caught in 'the logic of reproductive enactment' as 'the idea of habitus was underwritten largely by structural functionalist teleology; materialized in architecture and other spatial forms, it could only shape ideal subjects who would then reproduce the habitus in an almost hermeneutic circle' (1995: 572, see also Rapport and Overing 2000: 3). Returning to Butler's work, Morris shows how feminist gender performativity theory in fact departed from this to account for non-normative practice 'that may be embraced by individuals in courageous and joyously subversive ways' (1995: 573). By equating performativity more closely with the intentionality that might be associated with agency Rostas' description of the performative element of washing up allows us to see performativity as intentional 'consciously formulated' action not prescribed by 'practice'. Therefore the consciousness of the performative action might lie in either the actual expressive intent of doing the washing up itself, or in the construction of a wider strategic narrative within which washing up is organized temporally and rhythmically. One might also argue that performativity is an element of the repetitive – what Rostas calls ritualized – aspect of washing up if in doing the washing up in a particular way an individual repeatedly challenges established conventions. Such action transgresses and might transform practice by creatively shifting the parameters of traditional or established ways of doing things. It might also be embedded in specific emotional and embodied narratives, but yet in a way that is repetitive and in itself ritualized.

Rostas and Schieffelin both selected washing up as a hypothetical example. A focus on informants', often reflexive, descriptions of their own housework experiences and intentionalities allows a closer look at how expressivity as both reference and resistance to hegemonic gender, representations of self, and the experience of personal emotional narratives might intersect. For instance, those of my informants who had recently undergone changes in their lives described to me how the details of the way they washed up (for example the care they took, frequency, methods) had changed as their sense of self-identity underwent transformations. Washing up in a new way was for them part of establishing a new self. For some women this meant a feminist statement of resistance to the more traditional ways they had washed up and lived in the past. These might be established on leaving the parental home or leaving a relationship or flat share. Others self-consciously compared their own approaches to washing up with those of housewifely relatives noting that they did not wash up after every meal, or treated the washing up as a type of 'therapy' that they would engage in when faced with a problem when working from home. We discussed how their approaches to the sensory aspects of washing up differentiated their own sensibilities from those they associated with housewifely approaches. For instance one informant told me that after cooking a turkey at Christmas she had not been able to stand the grease to the point that 'I was so fed up of all the grease and stuff that I threw it [the baking tray] out in the garden in the end.' It remained outdoors for two days until she had 'psyched herself up' to tackle its greasy texture with boiling water – itself a sensory experience. Her treatment of the tray should be seen as an intentional conscious action carried out in relation to the sensory experience of a gendered individual. In this case the informant's method of washing up should also be understood as part of this emotional and sensory narrative; rather than an escape from the complexity of the consciousness of everyday life it was very much part of it.

Performativity and resistance are not simply located in the expressive detail of a furrowed brow, no longer rinsing the soap off or not drying up. Others informants emphasized the relationship between housework and their sense of well-being. In doing so they characterized their housework as subordinate to their personal non-housewifely narratives and in particular noted their own deviations from cleaning routines regulated by daily or weekly activities. This in itself constitutes a conscious re-contextualization of acts of housework even if they are repetitive. For example, Jenny, a university lecturer in her thirties lives alone. She has an active lifestyle, frequently travelling and socializing with friends, whilst also taking her academic research seriously. Jenny sees herself as having limited 'house-wifely' knowledge and says she does not have a regular housework routine:

Sarah: So you say you don't have a routine then?

Jenny: No, not every like people have a day for cleaning or, I sort of like do a little bit every day probably. It's this idea of maintaining it rather than actually going at it in full, that's why this whole massive spring clean was such a good thing probably.

Instead cleaning becomes more closely interwoven with her personal narratives in ways that might be seen as impulsive and that she characterizes as fulfilling needs that are essential to her own identity and sense of well-being:

Sarah: How do you feel about cleaning for you, is it boring or is it . . .?

Jenny: I find it quite therapeutic in some ways.

Sarah: Do you?

Jenny: Yes, definitely. Yes, I have this, like you were talking earlier on about this relationship to cleaning and I have this quite – but as I say it's never that, that thorough. It just is often a mixture of main-taining and then this massive clearout every whatever – three years. But I mean, I really, I don't know, I've felt so much better from having got rid of all that stuff, from cleaning it all out, I must say.

Sarah: So you're sort of like purging, aren't you?

Jenny: Very Catholic, yes. Oh yes.

Sarah: Do you think that's linked to being brought up a Catholic or is that taking it too far?

Jenny: No, it's not taking it too far at all.

Sarah: Really.

Jenny: No, when my friends came to see me they were all making fun and saying oh yes that purging, yes they were.

Sarah: I mean so how do you usually feel when the cleaning's finished then?

> *Jenny:* Ooh, purged. (*Laughs*) In Purgatory. No, I do actually. I feel, I really feel now I can go forward into the winter with all my cupboards clean.

Therefore housework might fit into an emotional narrative that is also an intentionally expressive statement about identity that transgresses hegemonic gender and practice. Jenny's example shows that although housework might involve the repetition of certain processes and actions these are done in a way that are both expressive and constitutive of *her* self-identity and feelings. Although anthropologically we might define this way of organizing housework as a type of routine, to Jenny's mind her housework is not done in a routine way as mindless drudgery. Rather it exemplifies her independence from the 'slavery' of routine. Indeed Jenny makes the housework serve her, using it as a therapeutic experience that will also create an environment in which she can go forward. Malcolm, who similarly says he does not routinely clean, also uses housework as a means to achieve ends that will serve and facilitate other activity at home.

> *Malcolm:* Yes, it's good to clean before making phone calls to sort of like prospective employers and, yes. It puts me in a frame of mind, an ordered frame of mind I suppose.
> *Sarah:* Does that show you something you feel about yourself?
> *Malcolm:* Yes, I suppose so, yes. I'm a more efficient, ready to communicate person.

Other informants in Spain who work from home and especially informants who had been students in the past also cited housework as a means of preparing emotionally for work or study. Angela, a working mother lived in Valencia with her husband and young son and daughter. She was often allowed to work from home two or three days a week. Unlike most of my Spanish informants, she found in her rejection of routine both a form of resistance to the housewife role she felt some expected her to play and an expression of self, for her housework was only secondary to her work – both a statement that she made verbally in our interview and also a principle she used to inform her approach to housework and the ways she would present her home to others. When I asked her what she would tell visitors who arrived when her house was untidy she told me: 'that I haven't been able to do it because I have to work, that I can't. Work is the most important.' She described how she would only clean before she worked when she was working from home because 'If I've got things very untidy then I have to tidy something up because if not I find it really hard work to work . . . If I've got to work I can't sit and do it at a dirty table.' However, as she pointed out, such cleaning would be done with 'the work in mind' and she would clean otherwise 'because I've got some time, I find myself more or less free from other tasks and I feel like doing it'.

These individuals give housework a place in their careers – which extend outside the home – and in their emotional narratives at home, seeing cleaning as 'purging' or helping one to create an appropriate state of mind to make a phone call, to do some writing, or some work. They describe how for them housework becomes part of an emotional narrative which is appropriate to their gendered identity. By doing their housework tasks at times that are not traditional, and for reasons that are not traditional, they are creatively placing these actions within emotional and temporal spaces that deviate from what they see as traditional forms. As Hughes-Freeland points out, however, 'Such performative diversity is not unfettered agency, but creativity contingent on a structure or a field of preconditions which constitutes a set of references' (1998: 7), in this case the spaces and actions that my informants associated with conventional housewifely approaches. This becomes a way of constituting a particular gendered identity in relation to the housework and in relation to traditional purposes of doing housework. This gender performativity need not be witnessed by an audience in all its detail and complexity in order to constitute a statement about gender identity. Rather it involves a creative process of expressing identity both to oneself, through its enactment, and to others, as it is recounted, through the display of its visual and sensory outcomes or through the confident and organized voice of a self that has performed and constituted a gendered identity that is now sufficiently formed to make a phone call to a prospective employer. Everyday performativity is therefore part of the process through which individuals' conscious actions are productive of their gender identities. This might be expressed through the actual practices of everyday housework and home creativity, or the wider context in which these tasks are undertaken.

My interest here is in how these everyday activities might then either maintain traditional gender roles and identities or bring about changing gender. Some scholars have argued that change cannot be driven by such creative individual acts. In particular proponents of sociological 'doing gender' approaches to housework here in recent times opened limited space for the idea of change through the transgression of practice. For example, Seymour (1992) finds 'men and women may construct a convincing rationale for performing a gender-inappropriate task which is actually performed for a pragmatic reason' that ascribes to the dominant gender ideology. She argues 'whatever the rationale, one of the unintended consequences of their actions will be to slightly erode the strongly gendered position of each task' but contends that this does not change the patriarchal structure in which domestic labour is carried out. Sullivan, still working within a sociology of housework frame, suggests understanding change by using a concept of 'gender consciousness' whereby people recognize 'rights based on information from the wider society' and actively generate these in social interaction. She sees consciousness as 'a critically enabling element in the transformation of the normative boundaries which regulate gender relations' (Sullivan 2000: 13). However, Sullivan's idea of a 'new cultural consciousness' involves individuals consciously plucking ideas from discourses (like the 'rise of feminism') that independently pre-exist. Thus the driving force is located in discourse rather than individual agency. In contrast Cohen and Rapport have suggested another way of understanding the relationship between individual consciousness, cultural discourses and social institutions, arguing that 'symbolic forms, institutions and forms' do not exist as ' a social fact somehow independent of the creative consciousness of the individual' (1995: 3). Instead individual consciousness brings culture and society to life. Acknowledging that such consciousness 'is limited by the forms and practices by which it can express itself and hope to communicate itself at any one time' Rapport argues that it is individual consciousness that 'is nonetheless responsible for animating those forms and practices with its own individual "energy" – its agency, intentionality and meaningfulness. Furthermore it does so in an individual – creative, idiosyncratic, ambiguous, situational, multiple – fashion' (1997: 7). This approach shifts the locus of change from discourse to the energy of individual agents. It implies change may be inconsistent, uneven, diverse and surprising, but it will be creative and driven by individuals' narratives and consciousness, rather than simply inspired by discourses and institutions. Indeed individuals may bring new meanings to the 'forms and practices' they 'animate'. Thus dominant discourses can change through 'processes of interpretation and reinterpretation' (Moore 1994: 83) that are brought to life, and given meanings, through the practices of creative individuals, for example by reorganizing how, by whom and when which knowledge, spaces and objects are used.

The Creative Imaginative Individual in the Material Home

The discussion above has demonstrated how individuals might produce their gendered identities through conscious and intentional performative action in the home and suggested this might be a driving force in the production of changing gender on a wider scale. However, a question remains since individuals are engaged in such activities in relation to specific physical material environments – in this case, architectural spaces filled with material objects and experienced through the embodied senses, emotions and intellect. In fact this is not solely a concern for anthropologists, but also for people who think through what their homes might 'say' about them. My informants themselves constructed relationships between self-identity and home, often drawing parallels between their projects of self-development and home improvement. To understand how my informants perceived the relationship between self-identity and home it is worth looking briefly at how people described their actions when they changed homes. On moving into new homes they often engaged in a process that was, for them, one of making the space they had moved into 'their own'. They described 'blitzing' or 'bleaching' their new homes from top to bottom, to eradicate signs of previous occupants or *their* dirt. This process of cleaning a new home is itself a sensory experience. Informants were likely to use 'strong' cleaners to remove the unknown dirt of strangers, producing at the end of their travail a sensory and symbolically clean space that no longer smelt of or was soiled by others. Once this 'clean slate' was established they felt ready, to use the words of one informant, 'to put our own stamp on it', to make it look and feel (i.e. also smell) 'ours' through home decoration, and display (visual, tactile and olfactory), by arranging furniture, and even making structural alterations. This process could be long-term, a series of impulsive artistic spurts, or might involve a period of living out of boxes while negotiating and deciding both with others and with the structure and design of the flat how their own stamp might be created in a particular shared architectural space. This perspective emphasizes the expressive work of incorporating a new home into a project of self and that might entail going 'against the grain' of hegemonic discourses (Moore 1994: 82) as one plans one's own use of a new space.

However, housework and home decoration are not only expressive and creative acts that exist in relation to convention and discourse. They are also contingent on individuals' relationships with their homes. The inter-subjectivity through which domestic gender identities are lived involves material objects, technologies and spaces, and embodied, sensory experiences. To some extent this involves the relationship between architectural forms, and hegemonic and contesting discourses. Studies of gendered use and symbolic organization of space have shown how built forms and interiors can be interpreted as representations of dominant or contesting discourses. Individuals' actions also constitute their responses to meanings they invest in domestic spaces and '[a]ny built form can serve interests for which it was not intended' (Dovey 1999: 183). Moore explores how people 'both consent to and dissent from the dominant representations of gender when they are encoded in the material world all around them' (1994: 75). She emphasizes how we use our living bodies to substantiate the 'social distinctions and differences that underpin social relations, symbolic systems, forms of labour and quotidian intimacies' in the 'material world which surrounds us' (Moore 1994: 71). Social actors become decisive because their actions may or may not invoke conventional cultural meanings associated with different parts of their homes. If they do not conform to cultural expectations then their actions 'may serve to confound the expectations of others, and thus potentially revoke or bring into question sedimented cultural meanings and values' (Moore 1994: 76). Moore suggests that 'actors are continuously involved in the strategic reinterpretation of the cultural meanings that inform the organization of their world as a consequence of their day-to-day activities' (1994: 76). As examples of such activities, housework and home creativity can be seen as actions that comment on discourses through conformity with or transgression of conventional uses of space or ways of doing things. This approach outlines how individual agency might be pitched against discourse and convention as it is represented in architecture and the expectations of others.

Other approaches focus on what Miller has called 'estate agency'. He notes that on moving into a new house one has to contend and negotiate with 'the pre-given decorative and other ordering schemes of the house' (Miller 2001a: 11). Indeed, when we look in more detail at how homes are created it seems that putting their own stamp on a new home is not necessarily a process of imposing a pre-existing stamp that each individual already possesses and which is expressive only of her or his identity. Rather this stamp is produced with (as opposed to *on*) the home. Other researchers have already begun to work on the relationship between the agencies of individuals and houses, often citing the agency of the house as a constraint to the agency of the individual. For example the contributors to Miller's (2001) collection reveal 'how far people are thwarted by the prior presence of their houses and the orders of their material culture' (Miller 2001a: 10). In favour of a stronger focus on the house itself, Birdwell-Pheasant and Lawrence-Zúñiga argue that individuals' personal agency might be weakened by a house but it is never cancelled. '[F]ocussing on the agency of individuals however, compromises our ability to account for the power of houses to structure and constrain the lives of these individual agents' (Birdwell-Pheasant and Lawrence-Zúñiga 1999: 8). The material culture and existing schemes of a house might influence the ways individuals can express their projects of self in their homes. However, individual creativity in relation to housing forms is also innovative and diverse; the materiality of a new home might constrain, or even provide a narrative for how identities are expressed in it, but does not dictate what is articulated.

Several of my informants had altered the structure of their homes, usually as homeowners with license to adapt an existing building to their needs. This included adding attic rooms to urban houses, and a porch or lobby to country houses. As their experiences indicate, both structural and decorative work in the home needs to be negotiated. Christine and her late husband had bought an English thatched country cottage to do up and had worked extensively on their home. They added rooms and moved the front entrance whilst maintaining the cottage image both internally and externally. Indeed Christine had felt driven by both her own identity and lifestyle needs and the character of the cottage as she worked in it. Christine described the choices she made in her kitchen in terms of both tradition and convenience, concepts that for her were perfectly compatible:

Sarah: Why did you choose this particular furniture?

Christine: What the timber? Because I think that fitted in with the place and I did do all the tiling though. I thought it was in keeping with the house.

Sarah: Did you do all that yourself then?

Christine: I did the tiling myself but someone came and did all the wood for us. We thought that that would save a lot of work later on. There's not much decorating to do is there?

Sarah: And what is it, what do you like about this kitchen?

Christine: I think it's very countrified, it's very convenient. I can come in and have a cup of tea, with a friend I've ridden with. It's nice to have a table. I do eat in here unless I have guests. It's just very homely and it's not huge but it's not small is it compared with kitchens today.

She had a similar attitude to her dining room:

Christine: We decorated this completely when we first came . . . They are the original curtains but they were on terrible old gold runner things so we've obviously put the poles up, which we think is more countrified.

Sarah: Is that quite important then to keep in the country tone?

Christine: Well I feel so, yes. I think gold modern things don't go in here.

In Andalusia Pedro and Susana had engaged in a similar project to develop an old family home into a convenient country house that they could live in. like They too had extended their home to include more bedrooms and bathrooms and they had also restructured their living area. Susana was also determined to respond to the old and traditional character of her home. She 'saved' the original fireplace and attached the cushions of the seating area around her dining table with antique iron nails. Her traditionally tiled kitchen contained a microwave, dishwasher and numerous smaller appliances. Susana's and Christine's projects in Spain and England involved careful responses to their own interpretations of the intrinsic and traditional character of the buildings they were restoring and reinventing, with the intent of creating modern convenient homes that were also in keeping with their rural location. They acted in their homes in ways that were negotiated with their material and sensory environments, but that also expressed their own self-conscious intentionalities. Moreover, although these two women of different generations (Christine was nearly sixty and Susana in her early thirties) living in different countries had very similar approaches to the creation of traditional, convenient homes, their everyday practices in them expressed their quite different relationships to traditional gender. Christine saw herself as 'not very domesticated', and had worked full-time throughout her life, whereas Susana engaged enthusiastically with homemaking and housework, feeling happy with the gender role segregation model that she and her husband work to as a fair way of dividing the different tasks that they need to accomplish as a couple. Creating a traditional home and responding to the demands of traditional design principles does not mean engaging with traditional gender. Therefore it is important to unravel the discourses and images of tradition people use for their own convenience. In Christine's case, the continuities between creating a traditional country cottage and her own identity and lifestyle can be seen through her outdoor work and passion for horse riding. Her approach ought not to be understood without the contributions of insights from 'horsey culture'. In contrast Susana's ought not to be understood without references to the symbols of traditional Andalusian culture replicated throughout her home.

Home decoration and decisions about how rooms and spaces might be used are thus influenced by individuals' projects of self, others' expectations, existing discourses and the existing physical composition of the home. These may all be seen as constraints on the way human agency is articulated in the home. However, these framing elements do not necessarily prevent change from occurring. Rather, they are points of departure to which individual creativity will refer, but is just as likely to transgress as to conform to. Indeed, as Christine's and Susana's examples show, they can give rise to apparent contradictions, as a house becomes both traditional and convenient. In the next section I discuss the idea of the incomplete home to examine how such creative individuals are implicated in producing not only innovative homes, but change.

The Incomplete Home

My fieldwork led me to conceptualise home as a necessarily incomplete project. Each of my informants discussed with me what they had done to change their home, what they planned to do, what they would like to alter, and/or what they would do if 'allowed'. Above I described how Christine and Susana restructured and decorated their homes in specific negotiations with their own perceptions of tradition, the existing structure and their own tastes and needs. However, as with all my informants, for neither of these women was the project of home complete; each had further plans and work that 'needed' to be done: new rooms to be added or further decoration to be carried out. In each of their imaginations, however close their material home came to their ideal, the home still 'needed' to be changed in some way that went beyond repetitive or restorative maintenance work. For some informants, structural changes would be necessary as they themselves aged, or home would in the future be re-made in a new space. These projects of home are not then necessarily circumscribed by one architectural space, but are better seen as projects that live in people's imaginations and travel and change with them through different spaces. Such projects may be compared to the homes 'in movement' (Rapport and Dawson 1998a: 27) of refugees and migrants who might carry the sentiment of home with them. In such instances Rapport and Dawson define homemaking as an activity for which people might utilize, for example, iconic architecture, clothing, routinized conversation, poetry or song (1998b: 11). For my informants, homemaking in the form of home creativity and housework was both emergent from and invested in a specific material architectural space, but never necessarily totally reconciled with it.

For those who did not own their own homes the disjuncture between the material and imagined home was more pronounced. When my informants felt a flat or house was 'not my style', or 'not me' the negotiations and contestations with this space and the human agents implicated (often landlords or flatmates) were articulated through innovative uses of space, organization of decorations and ornaments, or neglect. This could involve placing pieces of furniture in rooms they were not intended for, refusing to clean certain objects or do housework in certain rooms or spaces of the home, or 'just leaving' areas that one felt one has no responsibility for. When limited in the way they could decorate their rented homes visually by their landlords' requirements, people used different

ways of creating home, through sound and music, smell and reorganization. In doing so they found ways of living in spaces, which in identifiable ways did not correspond with their actual visions of home. In
addition to being a house or flat, home has a parallel life in the imaginations of those who live in a space they call home, but do not completely
identify with or feel entirely comfortable in. Home as an emotional and
imagined identity-space is thus never completed mapped onto the homes
that are emergent from peoples everyday living, housework and home
creativity. Instead the relationship between these two domains of home is
constantly renegotiated as the material and sensory home and individual
identities come into being. Although it might be possible to invest one's
identity in an architectural and material and sensory space called a home
it is rarely possible to do so completely.

Home might therefore be understood as a complex configuration of
identity that is closely interwoven with an individual's project of self,
and/or a couple's project of us. As a forever incomplete project, home is
never completely realized materially, but instead exists partially in ones
imagination as a series of constantly developing dreams or plans. This
perspective on the home helps us to see how the material and imagined
home are implicated in processes of change, and subsequently to incorporate these elements into a theory of the agency of the individual as a
driving force for changing gender. Rapport suggests the inconsistency
between imagination (derived from human creativity) and material reality
may be understood in terms of the 'gratuitousness of the creative act of
human imagination', which makes it 'inherently conflictual' representing
the constant tension between 'imagination and what is currently and
conventionally lived' (1997: 34). Thus imagination and the actions it
inspires in individuals can be seen as part of the conscious agency of
change – in Rapport's words 'moving to new possible futures'. The continuity of the conventional is, according to this perspective, only achieved
through successfully resisting such creativity (Rapport 1997: 34).

Thus the home and self can be seen as projects of the imagination;
projects that my informants could only imagine by using their existing
resources of experience and metaphor, gained through their interaction
with the world in which they live. When my informants described their
ideal homes they used the resources they had available, but were at the
same time aware there would be environmental (i.e. social, material,
sensory, economic) conditions with which this conscious construction
would need to negotiate. Effectively their projects of home were not
imposed by their environments, but were products of their existing reality,
which were created by their imaginations and would inform their future
actions. The home that would emerge in the future could not actually be

imagined as it had not yet come into existence; nonetheless informants could project their experiences to envisage and influence the future.

Individuals are certainly not free from the limits imposed by the material (economic and architectural) conditions of their lives. However, by distinguishing human from material agencies, with the former involving human consciousness and imagination, we can understand gender and home as products of the negotiations between these multiple agencies. Changing gender and changing homes are thus the material and performative outcomes of the relationship between human imagination and creativity, the resources of existing personal and cultural experience of each individual, and individuals' everyday engagement with their environments.

Summary

Based on the above discussion I suggest an anthropological approach to housework and home creativity that entails a series of conditions. First, gender performativity must be understood as a part of everyday life and action, as expressive and intentional, as both an element of and an elaboration on ritualized everyday action, stretching it and in some instances resisting or contesting hegemonic gender. Second, agency must be considered to be linked with intentionality, to be often self-conscious and part of performativity, but it must be recognized that this agency is not unfettered, it occurs in relation to the constraints of existing terms (or actions) of reference. To be conversant with existing (hegemonic) discourses and the constraints they imply, performative actions must be sufficiently recognizable on *their* terms, but because they are creative, expressive and transgressive, they might also stretch these constraints and be instrumental in processes of change. Third, individual creativity and imagination must be viewed as key forces underlying individual agency in the home both in terms of individuals' abilities to shape their projects of self and their projects of home. The creative and strategic actions informed by individuals' material and sensory environments, experiences and imaginations will become forces that serve to either maintain or transgress existing conventional gendered approaches to and ways of doing housework and home creativity. As such, continuity and change are created through everyday actions in the home, often in diverse and seemingly contradictory ways as individuals creatively reference, conform to and depart from existing realities.

–4–

The Sensory Home

In this chapter I continue the discussion of the relationship between gender, identity and home through a focus on the senses. In doing so I examine theoretically and empirically how people in Spain and England use sensory categories and metaphors to represent their domestic understandings and practices. As such they simultaneously make expressive statements about their gender identities in which are embedded moral commentaries.

The anthropology of the senses developed initially as a means of comparing the sensory classificatory systems of different cultures (e.g. Howes 1991, Classen 1993). Early work provided a background in how knowledge about the senses and sensory experience is organized differently in different cultures. However, it had little interest in individual sensory experiences and could not encompass the idea that individuals might breach the norms of their culturally prescribed sensory interpretations and actions. Subsequent work has shifted the focus to the relationship between the senses to emphasize their interconnectedness (Seremetakis 1994, Ingold 2000, MacDougall 1998). The phenomenological approach of this recent work assumes a different focus on varieties of embodied sensory experience within specific cultural and social contexts and on how people use metaphor to interpret and communicate about this. In this chapter I draw from both of these bodies of work. Towards the end of the chapter I compare Spanish and English sensory understandings and actions in the home. However, my interest is not solely in culturally constructed understandings of the senses but, following on from the previous chapter, in how individuals' sensory practices contest or affirm culturally specific gender discourses.

Connected and Separated: Talking about the Senses

Analysing how people describe their sensory experiences involves an inevitable contradiction. The sensory modalities of touch, smell, sight and hearing cannot be disconnected from each other in any essential way. Yet my interest is in how individuals classify and label their sensory experiences and actions by using specific sensory terminology. When my informants spoke about sensory experiences they tended to focus on one sensory modality at a time. For example, an old chest of drawers might be discussed in terms of its smell, although it could have been described in terms of sound or texture – for example, the jerkiness and squeaky noise when drawers were pulled out or the scratches on its surface. However, expressed as an olfactory problem an olfactory solution might be sought, such as spraying it with air freshener or inserting 'smelly' sachets with ones clothes. Concentrating on a particular category of sensory experience might also support an individual's development of a particular strategy of resistance or communication. In his work on the Songhay, Stoller has shown that by attending to such processes anthropologists might interpret how people develop strategies that make statements of resistance, using non-linguistic and non-visual means of commenting on (and potentially changing) their social positions. For example, Stoller's informant Djebo, a young woman who was discontented in her relationship with her husband's family with whom she had to live, used taste as a form of resistance. She intentionally prepared 'tasteless' or bad tasting sauce as a way of expressing her frustrations. Sauce, Stoller tells us, was a 'major ingredient in the stew of [Songhay] social relations' (1989: 15–34). Although food is also experienced visually and through olfaction and texture, here its taste was brought to the fore. Other research in non-western cultures reveals how people living in the same culture might privilege different sensory modalities in spoken accounts and practices. For example Desjarlais (2003) focuses on the biographical narratives of two elderly Yolmo Tibetan Buddhist people. He reports that:

> while Mheme's recounting of his life was dominated by motifs of vision and bodiliness, of knowing the world through visual means, and of acting and suffering through the medium of his visible body, Kisang Omu's accounts of her life largely entailed a theater of voices: when narrating significant events in her life, she often invoked, in vivid, morally connotative terms, the voicings of key actors in those events. (Desjarlais 2003: 1).

Such practices that might privilege other senses over the visual are also evident in the narratives of modern western informants. For example, in a biographical study in Britain Hecht describes how her informant, Nan, used images, sound, touch, smell and taste to evoke and communicate her memories. Hecht's text shows how Nan selected different sensory modalities to communicate particular memories. For instance, she used photographs, maps and drawings of her childhood home to objectify her embodied experience of housework and decoration (Hecht 2001: 134) and used smell and taste to evoke sensory memories of the past in 'Memory and Smell reminiscence sessions' in local community schools and museums (Hecht 2001: 140). Hecht shows how Nan's sensory practices were concerned with evoking the past. As I describe below, modern western sensory practices are also involved with the construction of the self in the present and the projection of imaginative and creative notions of the future.

By privileging different sensory modalities, my informants described home creativity and housework practices through which they expressed their gendered identities. They used sensory metaphors to describe practices that can be interpreted as performative statements of resistance and conformity that are ultimately manifestations of changing gender. In Chapter 3 I suggested changing gender is an outcome of the relationship between individuals and their homes. Both gender and home are mutually constituted through the engagement of individuals with their material, social and cultural environments. The performativity I associated with individual agency engages, and engages *with*, vision, sound, smell, touch and taste to perceive, create and maintain the home environment. However, different people take different sensory routes to what we might perceive as the 'same' sentiment or moral statement. For example, if two women shared a rented flat one might say her sense of home is created when she plays music and burns scented candles in the evening. The other may say she feels at home when she sees photographs of her family on the wall. Here, individual representations of sensory experience are my starting point. I shall interrogate them to understand how my informants' creation and interpretation of sensory experience and metaphor in their homes, might (like other types of performativity) reference, affirm or contest hegemonic gendered uses of smell, texture or sound, or be used to situate a particular gendered self-identity. Below I discuss metaphors of vision, smell, sound and touch separately. Then, through the example of dust, I examine how individual choices of sensory metaphors and practices in specific cultural contexts are expressive of identity.

Visual Display, Visibility and Future Visions

Most existing work on domestic material culture takes visual or visible aspects of home as its focus, concentrating on home decoration, arrangement and DIY. Early studies saw home decoration as a normative activity (Clarke 2001: 25), suggesting one might 'read' culture from the home as text. For instance Emmison and Smith draw from Bourdieu's (1990) study of the Kabyle house and Halle's (1993) discussion of art in the home to suggest researchers visually observe domestic decoration, objects and arrangements to 'decode' social norms and values (2000: 156–7). More recent ethnographic approaches (see Miller 2001a: 5) indicate that home decoration can neither be read as text, nor necessarily reflects normative values (cf. Clarke 2001: 29). Rather the visible or aesthetic qualities of home decoration (and housework) are the results of complex relationships between the different identities, agencies, resources and relationships in the home (e.g. Miller 2001b, Clarke 2001, Silva 2000). Visual home decoration is interlinked with the construction of the self in the present through selective biographical representations of the past (see Hecht 2001) and projections of an imagined future. By examining how women's fantasies of an ideal self are interwoven with their home decoration, Clarke characterizes the home as a process though which 'past and future trajectories . . . are negotiated through fantasy and action, projection and interiorization' (2001: 25). Visual home decoration is part of the project of the creative individual outlined in Chapter 3, interwoven with the process through which gendered selves emerge. This existing work confirms that visual home decoration and the arrangement of objects and furniture are important to the construction of identity. Here I want to extend this to the visual and visible aspects of housework. In Chapter 3 I discussed the relationship between decoration and housework. Both are concerned with visual and visible aspects of home, and housework is equally important in the 'aesthetic construction of home'.

Much of the effort my informants put into imagining, creating and describing their homes was concerned with display and visibility. They saw the visual as a means of self-expression and were confident that they could become knowledgeable about other people by observing their choices of objects and images and the cleanliness and tidiness of their homes. It was important to them to express themselves by decorating their homes, often using their own hands and imaginations, with objects that had personal meanings, in a style they felt was 'me', that represented their biographies, relationships or interest. The visual was also an important part of their approaches to housework. Visibility was key, although in varying ways for different people. My housewife informants cleaned their homes regularly to remove both visible and invisible dirt, and one of my Spanish informants had sacked her cleaner when she discovered she had not swept and dusted underneath the chairs and in 'hidden' nooks and crannies. However, non-housewife informants took different approaches. For instance the entrance area to Pilar's Spanish city flat combined various stages of her biography (she was about fifty years old at the time):

Pilar:	This is the entrance hall. If you like . . . This is from Italy, a trip to Italy and that's antique as well. That's from my family, a family painting. That's antique as well, and this is too.
Sarah:	And the tables?
Pilar:	They were a wedding present. They're antique but they're not . . .
Sarahr:	And this [an old school desk]?
Pilar:	That's from school. From the school I went to when I was little. I brought it here when I got married.

Pilar used these visible objects to draw together her childhood memories, key events in her life, and her passion for travel and education. When she spoke about cleaning she also used visibility to express her identity as a woman who had better things than cleaning to do. Pilar cleaned once a week. She would only dust something during the week if she *saw* that it was very dusty. Like other informants, her focus was on visible dirt, and she didn't clean every day to remove dirt that in her view could not be seen. Embedded in this approach were moral arguments about what is important in life. Christine lived in a large English cottage opposite her stables. She has a lifelong passion for horses. Her living and dining rooms and corridors were decorated with paintings, photographs and figures of her horses, dogs and family. She described what these meant to her, and how they fitted into her approach to life:

Christine:	The paintings, my brother bought this one for me in America and I've just, it's just come back framed. I'm very pleased with that.
Sarah:	What was it that you liked about it in particular?
Christine:	I think a painting is a very personal choice, something you feel you can live with. It will remind me of my holiday there and I just liked the style of the painting – it was very soft. I'd like to be there looking at it now.
Sarah:	And what about the others?
Christine:	The hunting scene I bought at the Norfolk show this year because I'm obviously interested in horses. I just thought that was quite pleasant.
Sarah:	You just enjoy shopping then?
Christine:	I enjoy spending my money yes. I try to work hard and play hard. This painting a friend of mine, who's obviously a very good artist, did. This is a horse that I had for a long time. Obviously in my younger days when I did hunter trials and it's nice to have the picture.

Christine's description of her paintings drew together a series of experiences and memories that related to family, past, present and an imagined recapturing of experience in the future. Like Pilar, as a woman who enjoys travel and outdoor activities rather than domestic life, Christine mapped out a part of her biography that spoke about where her priorities lie. Much of Christine's everyday life and social world involves horses and the community of friends who shared her interests, and it was unsurprising that this was represented visually in her home decoration. However, her attachment to a country and 'horsey' lifestyle was also manifested visually in other areas of her home. Christine joked about her bathroom, pointing out that, 'it's not at its best at the moment, there's a lot of straw on the floor', but commenting on how this was inevitable given that she worked with horses all day long and had to change out of her working clothes in her house. Although the straw was by no means an intentional decoration, Christine regards herself as 'not very domesticated', a very active person and not one to waste time. She usually accepted the reality of the sight of straw on her bathroom floor and waited for her cleaning lady to remove it. Not only visible, it formed part of the texture of home that cyclically accumulated and was removed. Christine referenced the moral discourse that straw should not be seen in her home by jokingly hiding it under the mat. By leaving or hiding it rather than cleaning it up she demonstrated that she was not prepared to be 'domesticated'. She used both the visual presence of the straw and the idea of hiding dirt from view to resist the values of conventional feminine domesticity.

For others, housework meant creating a visibly clean home that did not correspond with their notion of housewifely classifications of cleanliness. For example, Jenny, who almost apologized for her inability to allow visible dirt to remain in her home, told me 'you know what? It's usually once I see the dust – that's when I clean. Once it becomes visible I think yes, it has to go.' These informants were keen to state that hidden dirt was not a problem for them, in doing so rejecting what they saw as the housewife approach of women for whom it is crucial to go beyond visible dirt to seek and remove dirt that is hidden from normal view.

Both home decoration and housework contribute to how people intentionally create and maintain the visual/visible aspects of home. They also form part of their projects of home and of self-identity and might be understood as expressive statements that conform to or go 'against the grain' (Moore 1994) of different discourses and interpretations of tradition.

Olfaction, Creativity and Agency

The anthropology of the home has paid little attention to olfaction. Most work in this area has focused on cross-cultural comparison and non-western societies. For Classen, Howes and Synnott, 'Odours are invested with cultural values and employed by societies as a means of and model for defining and interacting with the world.' They argue that 'the intimate, emotionally charged nature of the olfactory experience ensures that such value-coded odours are interiorised by the members of society in a deeply personal way' (For Classen, Howes and Synnott 1994: 3). Some studies have engaged with olfaction and morality, however again this has been done within a paradigm of cultural systems rather than individual sensory experience (e.g. Bubandt's (1998) study of smell, disgust and morality amongst the Buli of Indonesia). These approaches rightly show how olfactory cultural knowledge might inform ritual and everyday practices. However, their emphasis on how people interiorize society's olfactory meanings denies individual agency to maintain or transgress the olfactory conventions embedded in local cultural discourses.

My informants were concerned with the smell of their homes and deliberately used plug-ins, air fresheners, fresh air (from open windows), scented oils and candles, and cleaning products. When they described odours verbally they used terms such as 'stale', 'smelly' or 'fresh'. Thus they used established categories attached to positive, negative and moral values to express their repulsion, pleasure, approval or disapproval. When we toured their homes together much of their communication about smell was olfactory. Some invited me to share olfactory experiences with them, using smell to communicate sensations and ideas. Others buried their noses in fabrics or bottles, using facial expressions and sounds to communicate their pleasure or distaste. They introduced me to the different odours that inhabited parts of their home, describing and sometimes demonstrating how they created, eradicated or combated them. They sprayed their scents and products into the air, held a product-soaked sponge to my face, or invited me to poke my nose into a smelly cupboard, giving me a sense of how they experienced olfactory transformations. This olfactory work involves creative practices developed in relation to the possibilities and constraints of the olfactory environments individuals live in. Like other instances of performativity at home, these practices might involve affirmation or resistance and statements of self-identity. Rather than passive consumers of the pre-packaged artificial smells that Classen, Howes and Synnott see as characteristic of a post-modern age of simulation (1994: 204–5), my informants were creative appropriators and mixers of diverse smells in their practices of home creativity and housework.

Olfactory home practices can be divided into periodic decoration, with burning oils, candles and plug-ins, and olfactory housework as the repetitive action of introducing fresh air, and using cleaning products. In the prologue I described how Maureen managed her olfactory home.

Maureen adored perfume and used smell as a way of creating herself and her home. She had a bedroom drawer full of perfumes, and on arriving home from holiday her priority was to make the house clean by recreating her world of smell and eradicating 'unclean' smells. Maureen spoke of smell in her home in terms of her sense of self as a housewife. For Spanish housewives smell was also an important part of the housework experience. Rafaela for example pointed out how she would never even slip out of the house to the shop for more provisions wearing the clothes she had been wearing for cooking because she 'hated' cooking smells. For her dirt was not just a visual experience but also olfactory, as she described: 'I can smell cleanliness, its inevitable. I go into a house and I see dust, and I smell the dust and I say: "There's a lot of dust here." I can't help it. I can't stand dust. I have to get rid of it. That's why I use the vacuum cleaner, because I can't stand dust.' However, concern for the olfactory state of one's home is not simply a housewifely dilemma. Women who departed from housewifely approaches to their homes also described the olfactory negotiations they entered into with their homes. They described how problematic 'mouldy' smells might develop, when for example laundry was left too long in the washing machine before being hung out, pots were left too long before being washed, and vegetable bits remained hidden under the washing up bowl in the kitchen sink. In other cases lack of smell became a reason not to clean, as Holly noted: 'The fridge never gets cleaned out but it never needs it. Nothing ever spills in it. You can't really see much in there but it doesn't, it never smells.'

Maureen's description of her olfactory home in the Prologue is revealing as she refers to her own agency as a creative mixer and producer of smell, but at the same time indicates the multiple olfactory agencies that compose her home – for example the 'musty' curtains, the dog. She could not prevent these smells – they were produced by the organic environment in which she dwelled. Yet she could intentionally engage with them and temporarily subdue them. While the olfactory environments individuals create in their homes might be seen as olfactory expressions of self-identity, individuals' self-expression might be constrained by the sensory home. Other informants also experienced the olfactory nature of their homes and objects in them as a 'given'. For instance for Cathy, an English housewife and mother in her thirties, a leaking airing cupboard that had become a bit smelly was accepted as part of the home, and for Julie the smell of a wooden chest that was remedied with perfumed items was something to be lived with. Using smell as a metaphor to discuss these areas of their homes, these informants also perceived their own agency to 'change' the smell of their homes, or part of their homes (albeit temporarily) as an aspect of their 'struggle' to create an appropriate atmosphere of homeliness. Thus it might be by performing an everyday practice of dabbing on some perfume and deodorant and opening the windows each morning, spraying air freshener when one gets home from work, or burning a scented candle in the evening, that both self and home emerge through individual creativity and engagement with the olfactory agencies of home.

Sound, Body and Everyday Narratives

Existing anthropological discussions of sound have been developed mainly in the work of Feld and in ethnomusicology. Some recent studies have demonstrated the importance of sound in modern western societies. For instance, Rice, following Feld's (1996: 97) notion of acoustemology as the 'exploration of sonic sensibilities' (Rice 2003: 4), has explored how a 'sonically constituted self' is produced in a British hospital environment. Rice's work demonstrates the importance of sound as knowledge in a context where, he argues, other (e.g. visual, olfactory, taste and, in some cases, tactile) sensory stimuli are suppressed or restricted (2003: 5–6). Here, my concern is with the less studied (with the exception of Tacchi 1998) area of how individuals use sound in their personal and private experiences of home and the sentiments this evokes.

Sound, whether intentionally created or not, is inescapably part of the home. This includes the sound, of speech and conversation, of music, radio, television, domestic dogs barking, uninvited bats squeaking, windows knocking against their frames in the wind, the running water and clanking ceramics of washing up or an intentionally slammed door. These and many other sounds are crucial elements of the way people communicate in their homes. My research focused more specifically on the use of music and radio in relation to individuals' everyday narratives and practices in the home. Several informants had musical instruments in their homes that they might play when alone or with friends, some informants played music CDs to me. We discussed how music and radio fitted in with how they experienced certain spaces of their homes and actions they performed at home when they were alone. Music was part of the embodied experience of housework as they danced while they dusted or burst into step as they cleaned the kitchen surfaces. Dancing during housework at home was a private and uninhibited act that they would have felt embarrassed to be caught doing. Yet it was simultaneously an intentional and expressive practice. For example, in England Nicola, who lived alone, told me that when she cleaned her kitchen she might start to dance, something she found 'natural' and 'uplifting', but at the same time embarrassing,

I think I'm some sort of ballerina or something. Some stupid jazz dancer. Yes that's what's so good about the house as well because nobody can see me in fact. This little thing I've pinned up here is actually a sarong that I made for going on holiday but it makes a fantastic blind, real cheap and basically from the outside no-one can see in.

In Spain Susana told me that when she was at home alone 'I spend the day dancing on my own in the morning ... I don't like gymnastics because I'm lazy. I don't like going out running either. But I love dancing.' This extended to her housework: 'Yes, I usually have the music on and I sing to it. It relaxes me. I have the music on and I shout, sing and dance.' Other informants equated cleaning with dancing, relating the embodied experience of moving to music to dance. Javier for instance told me that 'As I put music on when I'm cleaning, I love it. It doesn't seem like I'm cleaning; its as if I'm dancing. It's no effort.' For these informants, dancing and movement to sound was about performing the private self at home; although they also danced when out at parties or in clubs, here they combined a less inhibited dancing body with the embodied experience of doing the housework. This involved combining music they identified with and housework movements. For example Susana danced to traditional Spanish music that she loved and danced to at local festivals and parties, while Nicola danced to David Bowie who at the time was her dance role model. Combining music, movement and housework in this way enables individuals to connect their experiences of housework to other activities, thus incorporating it into part of the vision they have of themselves as individuals. Susana's experience of housework was linked to her taste for traditional song, dance and home decoration, and the gender role segregation model that she and her husband worked to at home. Significantly the traditional Spanish *Sevillanas* she danced while doing housework are danced in couples. Men and women have different roles and steps. Nicola's experience was connected to the dance styles she was currently exploring and the privacy she associated with her home, but was also part of her departure from traditional gender as she was an independent young professional woman. In contrast to the feminine dance routine that Susana performed, Nicola danced in the style of a successful male public performer. Thus by performing housework in a masculine dance style she broke the link between the practice of housework and the traditional femininity associated with it.

Each individual used music and other media (for example television to accompany ironing), in their home in specific ways with particular activities. Sometimes this would be to intentionally create an 'atmosphere'. In

England, Mario, who was in his twenties and lived alone in a student hall of residence, showed me how he put away his clean laundry to music, creating an atmosphere in his room that he enjoyed and saw as therapeutic:

> *Mario:* I go through phases of listening to various pieces of music and things. I recently saw the film Gladiator which is absolutely fantastic and I loved it so I got the soundtrack. So that looks very nice, classical. Quite stirring in places and very sort of ethnic Arabian chants in others so I shall put that on, it's quite quiet.
>
> *Sarah:* Is that something you might listen to?
>
> *Mario:* Yes, I like sort of, I'm very much into reflective calm mood music and I'll often put that kind of music on when I'm doing my laundry, rather than something faster. I find it almost a therapeutic process of being sat there and going through this laundry.

In Chapter 3 I described how Jenny and Malcolm used housework as a therapeutic process, incorporating it into their everyday emotional narratives as appropriate. Mario's use of music signified a similar process, a means of making housework serve him.

Radio sound also forms an important part of the home, sometimes including music, but usually offering a different type of 'atmosphere' and sentiment. The use of radio by both Spanish and English housewives has been mentioned in existing work (e.g. Oakley 1985, Gil Tebar 1992) and, as Tacchi has noted, radio sound 'contributes greatly to the creation of domestic environments' – it 'creates a textured "soundscape" in the home within which people move around and live their daily lives' (1998: 26). For my informants, different sounds were also associated with different rooms in the home. For example, for Andrew, a university lecturer who lived alone, listening to Radio 4 was part of his experience of being in the kitchen, and part of his sensory experience of activities he engaged in in his kitchen, whether he was cooking a meal, cleaning or just coming down from his study to make a cup of tea. As such it formed part of a sensory space he moved in and out of. His choice of radio station for the kitchen is also significant since Radio 4 is the station that is most likely to broadcast intellectual programmes and to interview other academics. The most domestic of spaces of his home, in which he would engage in the embodied traditionally feminine tasks of cooking and cleaning, was thus tempered with the most intellectual radio station available. In other cases, choice of radio station and programme was much more geared to the changing contexts and narratives of everyday practices at home. For example, Virginia, who lived with her partner in the countryside, described how sound fitted into her day and activities at home:

> *Virginia:* It kind of gets me going. I put the radio on when I'm having a shower and what happens really, it's quite interesting, he [her partner at the time] turns it over to Radio 4 during the day – cos he'll have a long soapy bath and he'll listen to Radio 4. I automatically turn it back to music stations. So once I've come back up here after I've had my breakfast in a morning, I switch that one on and it gets me going, you know, a music station as opposed to Radio 4. I might listen to Radio 4 downstairs when I'm having breakfast, but you know, by the time I get up here I want to really wake up. I know I've got to wake up cos I'm on my way to work, so yes . . .
>
> *Sarah:* . . . Do you choose specific music for the mood?
>
> *Virginia:* Yes, yes I do. I suppose I listen to classical if I'm feeling a bit melancholy. And some sort of other, I don't know, pop bands . . . stuff like that, but then I will choose . . . more sort of upbeat music if I'm, perhaps if I'm cleaning and stuff, and if I want to get ready for work or do whatever, then yes, it's got to be more upbeat music.

For these informants radio and music were closely integrated with their everyday emotional narratives and an assertion of the sort of man or woman they saw themselves as being. Used in combination with housework, music and radio are implicated in what people see as the therapeutic and relaxing processes of self-definition they engage in (usually alone) at home. Domestic soundscapes are personalized and expressive forms, created in negotiation with the existing sounds and silences that each individual hears in her or his home and the 'mood' or 'atmosphere' she or he imagines and aspires to. As Tacchi points out, they are 'established and re-established continually in each domestic arena, through each individual instance of use' (1998: 26). Domestic sounds need to be constantly maintained or replaced: the radio must be switched on and off, the programme changed, and CDs changed or re-played. This active intervention forms part of the everyday performativity of life at home, and the choices made are part of the process of living out a certain gendered self.

Tactile Homes

Despite the great anthropological interest in the material home, little attention has been paid to tactile experience and the texture and feel of home and domestic objects. The exception is Seremetakis' (1994) work on memory, commensuality and the senses in Greece which demonstrates how the textures of, for example, food and fabrics become intertwined with and evocative of memory. The textures of home are nevertheless central to the way domestic objects and practices are experienced. Although less transient than smell, the textures of home are not permanent – they are constantly transformed as objects and surfaces become dusty or soiled, are cleaned or washed.

Touch and texture were clearly important to my informants. One of the most obvious examples relates to domestic laundry. Texture is a constant theme in television advertising for laundry products, linking media narratives with people's expectations in a two-way process. It was in their laundry processes that my informants felt they had a strong degree of control over the texture of elements of their homes. The capability to determine the feel (and smell) of freshly laundered and ironed sheets on a bed and of freshly washed towels fell within the repertoire of domestic powers of my housewife informants. By revealing that they did not know how to achieve certain textures, or describing achiement of as a 'miracle' or 'mystery', was one way my non-housewife informants demonstrated that they did not possess, and moreover were not willing to engage with, the housewifely knowledge that informed such processes of tactile transformation.

As a material space, the home involves numerous potential tactile experiences. A clean cool tiled floor underfoot or the soft pile of a new carpet stroking ones toes, the bittiness of an unswept wooden floor or the stickiness of an unwashed kitchen floor, might all be experienced simply by walking around one's home. These are not essentially separate from the visuality of objects or surfaces, yet often my informants privileged tactile rather than visual experience when describing them. Some informants used metaphors of touch to represent their experiences of certain types of dirt. For example, Malcolm was concerned that his plastic kitchen floor should not feel 'tacky' underfoot: 'Any floor where if I walk in my bare feet after I've just got up, I pick up a layer of whatever has been cooked in the last week – that annoys me.' Similarly Juan noted the sensation of feeling that a tiled Spanish floor was dirty underfoot:

> If I'm barefoot and things start to get stuck on my feet then its time to sweep and wash the floor. With the dust, I like to be able to do this (wipes finger across the table) and see there's no dust, at least not any dust that you can see. In general I concentrate on the floor, not the dust.

By describing their relationship to their floor in terms of touch and feel underfoot these informants were using sensory metaphors that they were well aware would not be the metaphors a housewife would use to represent the state of her home. The housewife of their imaginations would not wait to feel a dirty floor underfoot. Most Spanish housewives sweep and mop their tiled floors everyday and although English housewives might mop their kitchen floors less frequently they would clean spillages or dirty marks as they occurred. Malcolm and Juan did not privilege vision in these discussions, not even pointing to the floor or asking me to look at it, as they were keen to emphasize that their tactile experiences had driven their decisions to clean. They identified their tactile experiences as the moment of their conscious knowledge that cleaning should be done. Like sound, images and smell, the textures of home and the everyday practices through which they are understood, created and maintained are implicated in the way individuals perform their gendered selves. Tactile metaphors provide them with ways of articulating gendered and moral categories of action, and the moralities implied in their maintenance of or resistance to them.

Sensory Metaphors, Cultural Knowledge and Self-expression

Above, following my informants' uses of sensory metaphors, I have separated the senses to demonstrate examples of how they are perceived and constructed through housework and home creativity. My emphasis has been on how metaphors of touch, smell, sound and vision can be engaged in representations and actual practices of home and gender. However, as I indicated at the beginning of this chapter, different people use different sensory metaphors to describe similar experiences and perceptions. My informants used metaphors strategically to express how their perceptions of their environments, and their relationships with their homes correspond to a particular moral worldview. For example Malcolm and Juan said that they understood that their floors needed to be cleaned through tactile knowledge, and used this as their personal gauge to determine the moment when they would clean. Indeed these informants recognize that other people would be prompted by a visual sensory cue to clean the floor, but are not prepared to engage visual knowledge in their own decision-making.

My informants used specific sensory metaphors to invoke moral and cultural values and their own maintenance of or resistance to these. The example of dust illustrates this well. My informants reported seeing and smelling dust. It was also referred to as a texture of home. It was described as a film, or layer, that one can run one's finger through to leave a line, or from which we can remove a pot to reveal a circle that has been protected from its touch. However, the repulsion with which the embodied sensory experience of dust was experienced varied according to the extent to which particular individuals rejected or accepted the moral values and knowledge about dirt that were promoted by sensory housewifely knowledge in their culture. Individuals' everyday attitudes to, sensory classification of and treatment of dust can be seen as instances of their gender performativity embedded in culturally informed notions of routine and spontaneity. Depending on what they considered to be the origin, composition and nature of different types of 'dirt', people tended to understand the need to clean differently and to use different sensory metaphors to describe dirt.

Dust was considered to be dirt by most Spanish interviewees. Above I described how Rafaela, a Spanish housewife, said she could smell and see dust, requiring her to remove it immediately. Likewise Manolo, a retired man who lived alone told me, 'Dust for me is obscene. It's unacceptable.' He described how he once visited a friend in Barcelona and was invited to stay for lunch: 'it was really dusty. Well, that day I ate three crumbs of bread and not much else. I was too embarrassed to say anything to my friend, of course. I can't stand dirtiness.' For most Spanish informants dust was thought to be dirt that rises up from traffic in the streets or from the land in the countryside, entering flats or houses through open windows and becoming a tangible entity as it collects on surfaces of the home. It could be produced by road works or construction work. For Carmen, a retired housewife, dusting was essential every day:

> *Carmen:* I see that the house is dirty when I go to bed, because you're looking at my windows and the square's all unpaved and a lot of dust rises up. When I'm going to bed I can already see it all full of dust, so here its every day, washing and dusting.
>
> *Sarah:* For you, is dust dirty?
>
> *Carmen:* Yes, like that there, I go in and see the dust and wipe it with a cloth.

For these informants dust, as a form of dirt that originated outdoors, crossed the boundary between street and home. The frequency with which dust was removed generally ranged between daily to once a week, though in some student flat shares it was infrequently removed. Given the importance of the distinction between home and street in traditional Spanish culture (see Corbin and Corbin 1984, 1986) it is easy to understand why for most Spanish people dust, as dirt from outside, should be considered problematic. As such, dust was not allowed to become a texture of home, it was removed as or before it became visible and tangible, and it was often considered to be 'repulsive' and to smell.

Those who resisted housewifely approaches treated dust differently. Some Spanish informants paid little attention to dust and denied that a house could become dirty within a few days. For example, Javier, who lives alone and only dusts on Saturdays, told me: 'A bit of dust on the floor, that's not so serious. I mean, the thing is perhaps you have certain structures that conceal the dust more, but if something's dusty it doesn't mean that its dirty for me.' Similarly Angela dusted about twice a week but, unlike most Spanish informants, not at regular times: 'If it's a bit more or less dusty, the house isn't clean, but its not dirty . . . Its not dirt. Within a few days of not dusting, you've already got dust, so its not dirt.'

English informants also considered dusting to be a necessary part of housework, but not a priority. Most saw dust as undesirable, but something that was an inevitable texture and part of the material composition of their homes. Attitudes of course vary in degree and some informants gave examples that emphasized their own resistance to what they saw as extreme approaches to dust. For example, for Christine it would not be 'terrible' if the house was a bit dusty: 'A friend of ours who is very house proud once ran their finger along the top of the door and my husband said "well you'll get a dusty finger" and that didn't bother me.' Similarly for Andrew dust was not a problematic type of dirt:

Sarah:	How do you classify dust?
Andrew:	It's if there's a layer of grey, which as you can see there isn't at the moment, but I haven't cleaned that – the piano – for about two weeks, three weeks.
Sarah:	And is dust dirt, to you?
Andrew:	Once I see it, and it's visible as a layer, yes. But I've got quite a high tolerance level to it.

Malcolm also set a limit based on the visibility and tangibility of dust:'I don't like visible dust, great sort of depths of it where if you pick up a coffee cup there's a sort of, the coffee cup hasn't been moved for about four weeks and there's a sort of ring. I think that that's gone too far.' For these men dust became a noticeable problem once it had formed visible layer and thus had become a tangible texture that could be manipulated. Pete, a single father whose adult children were still living at home, took this still further:

Pete:	Dust doesn't offend me unduly. I mean it gets dusty and I, you know, I don't see very well. Well I make this excuse to people that I'm short sighted. I'm sure I don't actually see dust the way other people do, you know. I don't spot it early.

Sarah: Do you think dust is dirt though?
Pete: I don't, no. It doesn't bother me. Dust doesn't bother me.

Pete invented excuses about his bad eyesight to pass off his lack of attention to dusting to his more house-proud friends and relatives, but at the same time represented his failure to 'see' dust as part of his having a different way of seeing or a different world view to them. Like Christine, he used his attitude to dust to differentiate himself from house-proud people.

While Spanish informants generally regarded dust as something that originated from 'outside', in England my informants understood this layer of grey as something that accumulated from inside the home, and moreover as something of themselves. They tended not to see dust as dirt. For most, dust was composed of dead skin cells – something informants reflected on and were sure they had learnt at school. This opinion is echoed in Margaret Horsfield's popular journalistic book *Biting the Dust*. According to Horsfield, the 'truth' about dust is that 'Although some household dust comes from dramatic sources such as volcanic eruptions and meteorites and some comes from obvious sources like building sites, concrete and roads, most of it comes from our own homes, from dead insects, from our pets and possessions, and from our very selves. Everything sheds little bits of itself every day: paint, wallpaper, wood, plaster, bricks, clothes, papers' and humans, who shed 'hair, dandruff and skin'. She continues: 'The *stratum corneum* – our outermost and lightest layer of skin – is shed completely every three days, letting loose some seven billion scales of skin, or about one gram, every day. In any home countless tiny bits of dead skin float around with gay abandon, making up a huge amount of household dust: up to 90 per cent in some estimates' (Horsfield 1998: 186). Thus for most English informants dust did not involve the intrusion of outside dirt and was seen as less problematic than it was by Spanish informants. As Jane described:

Jane: Untidiness doesn't bother me but uncleanliness does. So if it gets dirty, yes. I mean this wouldn't bother me, a bit of dust.
Sarah: Is dust dirt or not?
Jane: Well it's dirt, isn't it? It's dead skin cells, but its not really germs.

For Virginia dust tended to come from the open fire, but again it was not a problematic type of dirt: 'I don't mind dust, you know, dust is all right. That's not like dirt as such, although if it builds, then yes, I'll sort that out.' Similarly for Jenny dust was not problematic in the way that smells may be:

Janet:	I shouldn't, I mean I shouldn't like to think that the bathroom was dirty or smelly, or the kitchen or anything like that. But I'm quite happy with dust and cobwebs.
Sarah:	Why's that then? Why are they different?
Jenny:	I don't know. Because they don't smell, do they?

For most of my English informants dust was not a problem. It was a neutral texture, with no smell and that presented no risk. In contrast dirt that was brought into the home from outside was problematic and was either cleaned up regularly or avoided. Even for Allison, a part-time housewife and mother in her thirties whose self-esteem was closely connected to the cleanliness of her home and who followed a daily cleaning routine, dust was not classified as dirt. Allison suggested that if one scrutinized her doll collection one would find that their hair was dusty. For her, dirt was something that her children brought into the home on their shoes: 'No, I don't think it's dirt but, no, I don't know, no I wouldn't say dust was dirt. Or, I mean they don't wear their shoes in here you see so they never bring anything.' June and Graham, an active retired couple who were also relatively unconcerned about dust, made similar distinctions:

June:	Dust isn't dirt, is it?
Sarah:	Where does dirt come from?
June:	If we've been out walking and you've come back with your boots muddy, muddy socks, muddy trousers, it's been raining so your coat's wet, then you know you need to clean.

Similarly, although she considered dusting to be unimportant, Virginia felt it was necessary to clean her kitchen floor frequently: 'One thing that I do do most days is I sweep the kitchen floor and that's sort of like the catchment area of all the crap that comes through the house. Most people come through the house through the back door and if they bring stuff in, it sort of usually comes through the kitchen.'

Different definitions of the origin of dust, its material composition and the sensory embodied experience of it supported different views on the extent to which dust is problematic and the frequency with which it should be removed. A series of distinctions came into play here as my informants structured their definitions: between inside and outside the home; and between the self (as in dust emanating from the body) and other (as in dust originating from external processes). Whereas in Spain one could expect dust to smell because it is dirty, in England because it is of one's own body and produced through one's everyday life at home it would not smell. Both Spanish and English informants shared the idea of dirt as something visible and tangible that enters the home from outside. When dust was believed to originate from outside the home it was likely to be classified as dirt that should be acted on. These broad areas of agreement between my informants demonstrate how specific cultural knowledge and beliefs about dust informed their practices. Nevertheless their individual approaches to dust and its removal are also important. The extent to which dust is described and tolerated as a texture of the home is not simply an indication of response to cultural knowledge but also of levels of resistance to or maintaining of values and gendered identities through embodied practices within those cultures.

As the discussions of vision, sound, smell and touch have indicated, my informants used metaphors relating to each of these senses to generate and represent knowledge about their homes, and to intentionally create sensory aspects of their homes. These were sensory manifestations that they felt were appropriate to the gendered identities they perform at home. As much of our discussions focused on housework, informants explored how they might arrive at similar conclusions about the cleanliness of their homes through different sensory metaphors. However, this does not mean that their knowledge had been perceived through one, exclusive and separate sensory modality. We might separate sensory creativities, experiences and metaphors, as they are employed and constructed as a part of the performativity of everyday life. Nevertheless these everyday practices do not imply that sensory perception is separate and different for each sense. This means creating a balance between the anthropological analysis of informants' discursive uses of sensory metaphors that both construct and represent perception and experience, and the anthropological analysis of the home as a sensory world and experience.

The Sensory Home as a Context for Changing Gender

In chapter 3 I argued that theoretically we might understand that the home is produced through an intersection between the human agency of creative imaginative individuals and their engagements and/or negotiations with their everyday environments including the material, social, media, sensory and other agencies of their everyday lives. In this chapter I have developed this idea further to incorporate the idea of the sensory home. This implies that gender as it is expressed in everyday performativity, and thus as it comes into being, engages with sensory perceptions, experience and metaphors. Changing gender is thus also a sensory enterprise. The strategies of resistance, the stretching of the boundaries of hegemonic, dominant or traditional practices or discourses that people engage in at home, involve all sorts of sensory metaphors and devices. As the examples I have developed above indicate, these sensory strategies, like any everyday performative act, must reference and be conversant with existing forms of sensory expression and discourse, so that they might at the same time critique or resist these.

In the following three chapters of this book these understandings of gender performativity and the sensory home provide a theoretical and empirical context for my comparative analysis of the housewife and emergent femininities and masculinities.

5

The Housewife and Her World: Cultural Categories and Everyday Lives

In this chapter I discuss the notion of the 'housewife' and her relationship to the home through an examination of selected popular, social science and my informants' own representations. I situate the housewife as both a gendered icon and a lived identity in relation to the social, cultural, material and sensory contexts she inhabits. Existing approaches to the housewife have situated her symbolically, socially and structurally as isolated, oppressed and lacking self-awareness. These constructions of the housewife tend to deny her agency and diversity and do not attend to the sensory embodied nature of her relationship to her home. First I discuss some of these approaches. Then, drawing from my ethnography, I explore housewives' own experiences and how they are represented by men and women who do not consider themselves to be housewives.

Symbolic Analyses of the Housewife: Woman as Home

Existing symbolic analyses of the housewife situate her in terms of a series of theoretically constructed binary oppositions. Although such analyses are useful for understanding some cultural representations of domestic gender, they fail to account for everyday sensory embodied experience and diversity and do not accommodate change.

Morley, noting a well-established academic literature 'on the mutual identification of the woman, the mother and the home' (2000: 63), suggests the symbolism of woman and mother as home is key to C20 idealizations of home represented in UK popular current affairs programmes. In these, he argues, 'there is a collapsing of the image of the wife/mother into the image of the home itself' whereby 'The woman and the home seem to become each other's attributes' (Morely 2000: 65). Morley's argument implies that 'woman as home' occurs simul-taneously as a symbolic discursive element of 'culture', objectified in media representations, and as an experienced reality for contemporary women. He proposes that '[I]t is still undoubtedly true that at a simple material level, most women (and certainly married women) in the UK at least, notwithstanding their far greater presence in the workforce outside the home, are still more subsumed in the home than are men' (Morley 2000: 63) and that 'the place of the housewife is, of course, principally to make a home for her family', giving her responsibity for the domestic interior and housework. Drawing from Craik (1989), he insists that in spite of women's increasing participation women's lives are still split; at the centre of home life but at the margins of social life (Morley 2000: 73).

A relationship between femininity and cleanliness has been highlighted in such symbolic analyses of the housewife. Drawing from analyses of the meaning of dirt by Mary Douglas' and others, Morley concludes that 'femininity has been at least in part, defined by how women manage dirt' (2000: 78), seeing the housewife's role as to preserve the moral and physical cleanliness of the home, and thus to maintain its symbolic purity and integrity. McHugh likewise considers how 'cleaning practices interact with identity construction in modern bourgeois culture'. For McHugh, 'Cleaning, unlike speech, action, desire . . . belongs to a set of activities which confer an agency upon their subjects that usually *lacks* status and power' (original italics). Analysing representations of cleaning scenes in film, advertising and psychology theory, McHugh argues that 'cleaning practices and their representations participate in the construction and maintenance of vital cultural distinctions, like those between nature and culture, inside and outside, public and private'. She contends that 'the tropes, narratives, or sequences used to represent cleaning naturalize these binaries in such a way that they override or obviate other types of difference' and they do so through the figure of the housewife: 'in modern bourgeois culture, the linchpin (and alibi) of this process [of naturalizing binaries] is the housewife' in whom these binaries are 'wedded together'. McHugh's housewife 'symbolically polices, maintains and coordinates these binaries through her cleaning practices, and thus effectively embodies their contradictory juncture'. Thus she subsumes these contradictions under her femininity (1997: 18). These approaches suggest that the housewife's femininity is constituted through her cleaning practices, her maintenance of boundaries, and her ability to remain clean herself in spite of her daily contact with dirt. In doing so they deconstruct sets of modern binaries that inform and constitute discourses on difference, and the way these are used to denote status through references to cleanliness. These analyses also situate the housewife hierarchically. Morley claims not only a binary model of gender role segregation but (like McHugh) that the housewife is subordinate to the more powerful members of the household whom she serves.

Working with binary oppositions, modernity's traditional discourse genders the home feminine and defines the housewife's role as the creation and preservation of its moral and physical homeliness and cleanliness. However, whilst symbolic analysis usefully deconstructs *representations* of cleaning practices these are not necessarily descriptive of men's and women's everyday *experiences* of their gender identities. Morley and McHugh show how the relationship between women and home might be understood in terms of the gender binaries of traditional discourse, but do not offer an understanding of the complexities of women's everyday engagements with and creativity in their homes, or of the multiple masculinities and femininities that might be constituted through their domestic practices. To understand the status of the housewife it is crucial to acknowledge contemporary discontinuities between theoretical uses of binary dichotomies, the traditional discourses embedded in cultural representations, and how continuities and change are constructed by individuals and constituted in the diversity of everyday lives and actions.

Depressed and Oppressed: Contemporary Spanish Critiques of Traditional Gender

In Chapter 1 I discussed anthropological accounts of changing Spanish gender. Here I explore three contemporary responses to traditional gender, each of which suggests a departure based on women's empowerment.

In a volume about the changing status of Andalusian women (Sanchíz, 1992), the Spanish anthropologist Gil Tebar represents the everyday life of 'Maria', a 'traditional housewife', ironically and critically. Maria's everyday life and responsibilities are described from morning to night. Before showering herself, Maria first makes the family's breakfast and does the previous night's washing up. As her complaining husband leaves for work she has to follow himout of the flat to ask for housekeeping money. In the morning her daughter (a student) helps her complete her daily cleaning routine of dusting, sweeping and mopping the floors, making the beds, tidying her son's bedroom and cleaning the bathrooms. She showers, goes shopping and gets home to finish cleaning and cook lunch, taking a five minute coffee break at 11.00. After lunch while the men have a siesta Maria and her daughter wash up. Maria then goes out to buy her son's medicine, does the laundry and ironing and attends a neighbourhood meeting. By the time she has finished the meeting her husband is home and watching football on TV with his friends. She makes dinner, and after eating chats with her husband while they wash up together. When she has finished off in the kitchen he calls her to watch the TV film; she relaxes on the sofa and falls asleep.

Contemporary Spanish women *do* live with the legacy of the patriar-chal discourses and institutions of Franco's dictatorship. As Brooksbank Jones insists, there are indeed some fundamental inequities in Spanish society (1997: 73–94), and in Spain '[m]ost women's lives are very differ-ent from those of most men' (Thuren 2000: 172). Gil Tebar's account is intentionally critical; we are meant to notice that Maria's husband is irri-tated by her request for housekeeping money, that she continues her chores while he watches TV and socializes, and that she falls asleep, missing her film, as soon as she relaxes. Such daily routines *are* lived out by many traditional Spanish housewives. However, I would suggest that Gil Tebar's account represents not the experienced reality, or the voice of oppressed Spanish housewives, but a feminist argument that has a stake in the idea that change must be implemented. Nonetheless hers is not a lone voice; critique of traditional gender and directives for change are popular in Spain.

Carmen Alborch was the Spanish minister for culture and is author of *Solas* (1999), a book about, amongst other things, the dilemma of contemporary women striving for independence, freedom, love and companionship. One of Alborch's themes is the contemporary adage that one is lonelier in a loveless marriage than living alone accompanied by good friends. She describes on the potential that women have to live, cope and be fulfilled alone, arguing that contemporary women can and do have a choice. Within this scheme the housewife is a prime candidate for loneliness. Alborch outlines how housewives who have little contact outside the home, suffer from depression and feel isolated and that their lives have lost their meaning when their children and husband go out to do their respective tasks, and how the house becomes a space that restricts them rather than bringing them self-awareness. This, Alborch suggests, is also related to architecture, as the way living spaces are configured (above all in big cities) is not designed to improve women's quality of life, but is led by economic factors. Thus Alborch's housewife, forcibly isolated and simultaneously invaded, finds (if she gets them at all) her space and time difficult to value (1999: 214). Ironically accord-ing to Alborch, who has 'a friend . . . who, when she was married, used to shut herself in the bathroom because it was the only place where she felt free' (1999: 215), though the housewife is isolated in the home, she is denied her own space and privacy because 'the traditional housewife organizes domestic space to serve the needs of others and not her own . . . effectively many married women do not have any personal space because the size of their homes does not allow this, making them constantly available to others, and at the time same feeling trapped' (1999: 213–14).

Alborch's 'lonely housewife' is constructed to counterbalance the idea that women who live alone are inevitably lonely, and fits her argument that it is not women's marital or family status that determines the extent of their loneliness and lack of fulfilment, but their level of control over this status. Thus she situates the Spanish housewife in a scheme that deconstructs traditional gender relations to characterize housewives as trapped, isolated, unfulfilled and lacking self-awareness. This discourse, represented by a prominent Spanish woman, in a book that reached its fifteenth edition within five months of publication, argues for a departure from traditional gender, in the name of women's increased autonomy.

The idea that women should be taking greater control of their lives is also implied by a recent anthropological/psychoanalytical project. *Mujeres Invisibles* (Martinez et al 2000) is a documentary video that, according to its synopsis

> interweaves the life stories of six women aged between 26 and 88, in Cordoba, Spain. They talk to the camera about their own experiences and their silent everyday struggle to improve their living conditions and give their children a chance in life. Above all they see themselves as 'fighting mothers'; it is through these experiences that they construct their own gender identities, and represent themselves to other women.

Mujeres Invisibles was made by anthropologists in collaboration with local women and linked with a wider participatory action research workshop (Taller de las Cuatro Estaciones) focusing on gender identity and desire (Camas, Martinez and Munoz 2000: 46–7). *Taller de las Cuatro Estaciones*, the book accompanying the workshop (Martinez 2000), implies there is something wrong with the traditional situation of women in a patriarchally structured Southern Europe. This project set out to facilitate local women's self-empowerment by working with them on topics of gender and desire to encourage their self-awareness as a vehicle upon which they might initiate their own journeys of discovery. In *Mujeres Invisibles* the six protagonists, women from poor areas of the city, speak openly about their lives as women, what they have learnt, what they are now prepared to accept, and what it is to be a woman. The documentary gives a voice not only to the project but also to the women who participated in it. Importantly it departs from representations of women as housewives to explore how individual women articulate their own gendered identities, allowing them to emerge as creative and active agents.

In different ways these three approaches argue that traditional Spanish gender is at the root of women's isolation, depression and disempowerment. They call for women to have greater involvement outside the domestic sphere, to become aware of their own desires and needs and in doing so to bring about change. Whilst only Gil Tebar focuses on the housewife in detail, each of these projects implies that her status is problematic. However, curiously assumptions about the housewife's passivity appear to be at the root of each of these critiques (and correspond with the model of feminine passivity in traditional discourse on Spanish gender). As I have argued elsewhere, this denial of women's agency might be misleading. For instance some of the Cordoban women who Martinez collaborated with (see above) were in many ways disempowered (in terms of economic and social capital), but had successfully fought to change their lives to some degree. They had made choices and followed them through. The models of the Spanish housewife discussed above form an important critique of traditional gender. Nonetheless, problematically they also construct a reality for the housewife that denies her agency or fulfilment, and assume she is disempowered.

Bored and Disadvantaged: Studies of the Housewife in Britain

In the first important sociological study of the British housewife, Oakley argued that housework might be defined as 'work'. Using this analogy she explored the experiences and feelings of forty London housewives, interviewed in 1971. For her informants, 'Autonomy is the most valued quality of the housewife's role', however Oakley argued that this value was negative, rather than positive as 'The impression is given that, rather than being *positively* valued for its autonomy, housework is *negatively* valued as a retreat from a disliked alternative – employment work' (1985: 42). Oakley claimed that 'In the housewife's case autonomy is more theoretical than real. Being "your own boss" imposes the obligation to see that housework gets done. The responsibility for housework is a unilateral one, and the failure to do it may have serious consequences' (i.e. the 'wrath of husbands' and 'ill-health of children') (1985: 43). This, coupled with Oakley's finding that housework itself was the 'worst' part of being a housewife for her informants, added to the irony of autonomy: 'The housewife is "free from" but not "free to". That is she is exempt from supervision, but not wholly free to choose her own activities' (Oakley 1985: 44). Like Alborch, Oakley also identified isolation as a key problem for the housewife: 'research has shown that loneliness is an occupational hazard for the modern housewife, who is often not only cut off from community life but from family life' (1985: 88)

The analogy between housework and work continued in academic debates. The first edition of Malos's *The Politics of Housework* (published in 1980) was concerned with the question of 'whether women should be paid "wages for housework"' and was 'set firmly within a socialist feminist and broadly marxist perspective' (1995: 208). Malos argued against the payment of wages for housework, instead promoting an alternative political strategy based on a refusal to accept the idea of that the 'division of labour' was 'natural' either inside or outside the home and putting 'forward an agenda for personal and collective action embracing change both within families and personal relationships and in the public arena' (1995: 208). Malos lamented that by the mid 1990s 'it is obvious that the major struggles have not been won. Women play a larger part in the labour market than ever before, but are still in a disadvantaged position' (1995: 209).

In these characterizations the housewife is in an unhappy position in terms of her everyday experience of boredom and isolation, and situated in a political structure that naturalizes her femininity. Her passivity is emphasized above her agency as she is described as restricted both by architecture and society. However, more recent work has shown housewives engaging more actively with both the social and material contexts of domestic life. Silva, disputing 'Bourdieu's (1998, 1999) view of women within the long-lasting habitus of male domination', has argued that women might become 'active agents in the family and its consumption practices' (2000: 24) and thus 'operate as conscious agents of change in the sphere of intimacy' (2000: 25). The housewives Silva describes (some of whom also worked for wages outside the home) were both responsible for creating as well as caring for the domestic, family worlds in which they lived in their homes. Silva focuses on the importance of 'emotional capital' – 'a capacity to connect, involving acts, intentions and sentiments. It refers to moral thinking about personal connections and intimate life, related to the self and others. It is an essential ingredient for a reflexive self'. These are the 'invisible' labours of 'caring', which is 'a deeply devalued social activity' (Silva 2000: 4). Silva shows how her women informants sought to achieve social inclusion through acts of material consumption (of home domestic and media technologies). To do so they 'followed particular capital –accumulating strategies based on their emotional capital' (Silva 2000: 24). In Silva's account rather than being isolated, unconnected and acted *on* by their material environments, women in situations of economic scarcity used their emotional capital, resourcefulness, and social networks to accumulate home technologies that signified their family's social (and class) inclusion through their consumption. In such projects of home transformation housewives might take centre stage, not simply serving their families, but actively creating their worlds through a series of social and material relationships.

Lonely and Powerless?

The approaches to the housewife and housework described above (with the exception of Silva and, to some extent, Martinez et al) problematize the housewife and her identification with housework and the domestic sphere. They identify a theoretical and structural situation where space and activity are gendered and construct the housewife as disadvantaged, depressed, oppressed and lonely. She serves her family rather than her own desire, and, confined to the home, inappropriate architectural structures isolate her from a social world. In Chapter 3 I suggested women have more agency than such models allow; rather than merely oppressed by the buildings they live in, they might resist and reinterpret these material forms. Whilst symbolic analyses might read traditional gender ideologies as embedded in the social and material environments housewives inhabit, this does not mean that such buildings and relationships necessarily constitute housewives' oppression and isolation. Focusing not only on architectural forms, but on the full range of sensory experience and practice that mediates housewives' relationships with their homes and families, indicates that although some housewives' experiences include oppression, isolation, depression, loneliness, and disempowerment, these need not be conterminous with the identity of the housewife. Such sentiments are not *necessarily* an element of her femininity or of her relationship with her material and sensory home.

The following sections discuss my informants' notions and experiences of being housewives. I focus on how traditional femininity is situated in my informants' lives and on how the material and sensory home is implicated in this relationship.

(De)Constructing the Spanish Housewife

Academic and popular representations of the traditional Spanish housewife's lot make a strong case for change. However, Thuren (2000), Martinez (2000) and (Pink 1997a) have shown that contemporary Spanish women embody many forms of femininity. Some contemporary housewives are 'getting out' to participate in *barrio* movements, self-awareness workshops and documentary videos, and have different individual needs and desires. Being a housewife in contemporary Spain is not necessarily equal to being disempowered and miserable. I interviewed two women whose daily routines paralleled those of Gil Tebar's Maria, but who described their experiences in different terms. Lola and Carmen, two Madrid housewives, enjoyed housework. For them its daily completion was a means of living a role they aspired to and creating and maintaining the home they felt comfortable in. Like many working-class women (see Brooksbank Jones 1997: 73), Carmen had to work throughout her life in a variety of paid domestic jobs. Now in her retirement, being able to dedicate her life exclusively to being a housewife, caring for her home, husband and three adult children, was the realization of a life-long aspiration.

> Most of the time I get up early, tidy up the house, clean the house and then put the washing machine on, cook and in the afternoon, do the ironing, sew, and that's my life ... Sometimes I watch telly, and sometimes I nod off, normally when I'm watching telly, and then later on I do my sewing, the ironing, then I finish up. I get ready and go out walking for an hour.

The completion of her daily routines – of tidying the home and cleaning its surfaces, shopping, cooking and washing up a multitude of pots and pans and plates whilst her husband and son had their siesta – was a way of living out, of enacting and confirming, the status she had achieved. There is no ironic intent in her reply:

Sarah: What do you do for fun?
Carmen: Nothing. My fun is being in my house or going to my children's houses. That's my fun.

Lola was married, in her fifties, with two grown-up sons who lived at home and another who was married. She worked part-time as a housekeeper and dedicated her afternoons to her own housework, something she felt she had studied all her life, and was integral to her relationship to the material and sensory environment she enjoyed. Lola said she 'loved' how hot water enhanced the smell of her cleaning products, forming part of her familiar sensory world. Lola worked in another family's home in the morning, arrived home to cook lunch for her sons and husband and spent the afternoons doing housework. Lola showed me her bathroom.

Lola: Look, the bathroom. Look how they've left it and I had it all tidy. It's, they come in and they mess it all up.
Sarah: What have they done to mess it up?

Lola:	Well, one will have had a shower, the other one's had a wash. And I put the bathrobes away, if not . . . That's the way they go about things.
Sarah:	So, for you the bathroom's dirty?
Lola:	Yes, for me it's very dirty. Can't you see the foot prints? Can't you see them? They come in with their work boots on, and as they're filthy, well.
Sarah:	So now you have to clean up.
Lola:	Well, I'll do a bit before I go to bed.

I was struck by the continuous 'dirt' that Lola's sons created for her to clear up. But in Lola's world this did not signify her oppression. For her, cleaning was an enjoyable emotional as well as olfactory, embodied experience:

Lola:	For example, I really like hot water, so I use it a lot. It gives off a smell, so when you clean . . .
Sarah:	What does it smell of?
Lola:	Clean. Well, at least to me, it smells clean. It's something that I enjoy doing, that's the truth, although I nag my sons, because I like them to be clean and have everything tidy.
Sarah:	Is one of the reasons why you enjoy cleaning, that you like the smell?
Lola:	I like the smell, and I like to have everything clean.

It was important for Lola to be able to do her housework 'Because while I'm doing it, I feel active, I feel good.' She appreciated the products she used. Pouring a drop of one product onto a sponge she gently massaged it to show me its smooth texture and held it up to my face so I could smell its pleasant fragrance. Having worked as a cleaner and housekeeper since she was a teenager, she was an expert, and unapologetically proud of her expertise and achievement. Her daily work was inscribed on her body as she showed me her nails:

Lola:	Look at my nails. That's from working every day . . . I paint them once a week. I always have them . . . but . . .
Sarah:	But does the varnish stay on?
Lola:	Yes, but because I did them again yesterday. If not it would have worn off. The products eat it away, and from washing up, and everything, it comes off. Because sometimes I say, they're so long, they look lovely, and two days later they are soft from using so many products, because, like it or not, the anti-grease, it must contain caustic soda, or something like that, and in the end they break, you never manage to grow them. I have to put up with it, because I can't have them long, that's why.

One might propose that Lola and Carmen are constrained by a patri-archal structure and have a false sense of consciousness. However, having listened to their self-conscious accounts, I would argue that they have a choice. Their lives are intimately interwoven with the multiple agencies of home and part of their business is to maintain a material and sensory equilibrium, or pattern, at home. Their negotiations are not only with their husbands and children, but are also played out in relation to the struc-tures, objects and their sensory embodied experiences of their material environments. Lola does not have to burn off her nail polish with frequent use of products, or miss out on afternoon outings because she is cleaning at home. Carmen emphasized to me how she had steadfastly stuck to her routine, throughout her life, in spite of her husband and now her grown-up children asking her to go out. Indeed difference is part of Carmen's self-representation as she recognizes that different women have different priorities. Whilst it might be argued that women like Carmen and Lola do not have time to do things for themselves, consider Carmen's feelings about what *her* things are: 'The first thing I do in the morning is my things, whatever day it is . . . . the house is first, my bed and my things.'

When other Spanish women informants described housewives like Carmen and Lola, they did so in terms of their agency rather than their passivity, suggesting they are 'obsessive'. Lola's daughter, Lolita, described how her mother imposes her values on her underwear:

The thing is, my mother is a real obsessive about cleaning. For example, my mother when she's doing the ironing, she goes over the top, she even irons the knickers. When I lived at home the lace on my knickers was getting worn out from being ironed so much, because she's got to have them all nicely ironed. But as it's her that does it, we can't complain.

Ana, a single mother with three teenage daughters who worked full-time, also felt she had departed from the obsessive daily routines of her mother to some extent. She remembered that her mother had been able to see marks, that were never visible to Ana, on a spotless white door, and told me that 'My mother is obsessively clean and when I was living with her I thought she was mad, and paranoid.' But Ana also felt she had some of her mother's values because, 'you find yourself doing the same things as she does and you say, I can't believe it. So I don't think of myself as obsessively clean, but you're much more comfortable in a clean and tidy house.'

These women felt they had made a choice, and thus indicated that their mothers also had an alternative because there is more than one way to care for and clean one's home. Pilar, a music teacher with a passion for travel, lived with her daughter in her own three-bedroom flat. In her opinion there *was* a choice and she had made hers. 'I notice the dust, *if* I notice it, I'll go and clean it. But my system isn't to get up and do a bit of cleaning, not on Sundays either. My neighbour, she does. She works and everything, but she gets up, mops the floor and cleans everything. I get on with my life and I don't see it.' When I asked if she worried about what other people thought about the cleanliness of her home she told me 'I don't think about it, I really don't. I don't think about it, I'm not obsessive.' Pilar has decided not to do routine housework but to clean when it comes 'naturally'. Whilst she criticized her neighbour who 'lives to clean', she rejected the idea that the traditional obsessive housewife was a dominant gender identity in the contemporary Spain she inhabits, seeing her as mainly 'a thing of the past'. Pilar had a cleaner, upon whom she depended for expert housewifely guidance. Whilst Carmen set her practices in a narrative of difference, Pilar understood hers in terms of a process of change. For other women, resistance was played out in contexts of conflict. For example, some women, whose priority was not housework, felt their husbands' more traditional families criticized their approaches. Sometimes they self-consciously performed their rejection of a traditional housewife role to express resistance to *their* expectations, that for instance they should iron their husbands' shirts or take fuller responsibility for housework.

The traditional housewife is alive and well in Spanish culture. She is an icon that has been critiqued and abused, aspired to, relegated to the past and loved. In Chapters 6 and 7 I explore her impact in the places where she is absent to discuss how contemporary Spanish women and men live in their homes in relation to her, and the status of the knowledge and expertise that she stands for.

(De)Constructing the English Housewife

The English research allowed for a stronger focus on housewives' self-perceptions. In the Prologue I described how Maureen lived out her housewifely identity and morality through her sensory home practices. Along with Maureen, I also interviewed ten housewives living in nuclear family contexts, most of whom worked part-time. These women shared similar visions of the 'good housewife', how she would organize her domestic life and what she 'ought' to do. While I would not frame Maureen as *the* ideal housewife, her priorities, if not her full range of sensory practices, broadly matched the ideal these women volunteered. They outlined a series of activities that they thought they 'ought' to do and referred to knowledge that they 'ought' to have. For instance in the case of laundry my informants agreed that they ought to wash items as soon as they were soiled, check pockets, turn clothes the right way out, read and obey washing instructions on labels, separate coloured, white and black clothing, wash different items on different temperatures, iron as soon as the laundry was ready, and put laundry away straight after ironing. In a few cases this was expressed in informants' accounts of how they lived out their everyday domestic lives, however most were not prepared to engage with all the activities and knowledge that they thought a good housewife would engage in and our interviews were riddled with confessions about what they 'knew' they should do but did not, and about occasions when they had been 'naughty' and not obeyed manufacturers instructions, or overloaded their washing machines, or lazy, and not done their ironing, and so on. Using the technologies and objects in their homes as silent companions in their conspiracies to cut corners, these housewives abused their washing machines and mistreated their families' clothing in ways that were fundamental to their understandings of their self-identities. These women felt their own systems and the knowledge they used were sufficient for them to achieve the sensory results they wanted without engaging with the more expert knowledge and techniques appropriate to their task. They prioritized being a good parent over being a good housewife, rejecting the idea that housework might take priority over time with their children. Mothers organized their domestic routines so housework would be done behind the scenes and not impinge on family time. These women saw themselves as housewives, but did not want to live up to the image of an obsessive housewife – whilst they spoke of what 'you ought to do' it was part of their self-identity not to do all those things.

Whilst some housewives I interviewed claimed expertise but did not always use it, men and women who did not see themselves housewives, or as possessing housewifely knowledge, discussed the role of a housewife figure in their lives. Mario lived in a student hall of residence. He worked full-time as the President of Derby Student Union, whilst launching his freelance writing career. Mario's representation of his approach to housework was intertwined with his representation of his mother, her housewife role, knowledge and expertise. He claimed to have inherited something of her approach:

I can't go out with a scruffy girl. You know, I mean I'm not as comfortable. My mum's a bit of a snob, my grandmother's a big snob and I have inherited a few traits of that. I don't look down on people because personality is absolutely everything but if I'm going out with a girl and I'm going out publicly with her or she's going to meet my mum or you know go out with my friends I don't want her to be what I term as badly dressed.

Mario felt he had 'got on' with doing his own laundry because the necessity for having nice clothes was already part of his life; he had been brought up to be used to having clean clothes and a clean home: 'When I lived with my mother I used to put the clothes in the washing basket and miraculously within two or three days they would turn up again. Fantastic!' But Mario, like other men and women, felt unable to engage his mother's housewifely knowledge as his own knowledge (this is discussed in detail in chapters 6 and 7). For example, Mario considered the problem of a marked jacket; its washing instructions did not correlate with his usual laundry process:

> *Mario:* So I probably won't do it myself. I'll be moving all my stuff back to my mum's house and, bless her, she can do it.
>
> *Sarah:* Why's that?
>
> *Mario:* Well because she's my mum. She's got that special mum power when it comes to washing. My mum always got my washing right and you know I never had a problem with my washing. I always had confidence my mum was going to sort it out for me.
>
> *Sarah:* So you think that washing that jacket might require your mother's expertise?
>
> *Mario:* Well, partly it's laziness. Partly it's laziness but partly it's expertise. You know she's got mum power and she knows what she's doing whereas I don't really know what I'm doing. So she'll have to have a go at that.

Thus Mario elevates his mother's housewifely knowledge as something almost mystical – that he cannot understand. 'Mum power' is gendered power, not only linked to housewifely knowledge, but used by Mario to construct a binary opposition that he justifies by treating gender as a natural given. He constructs a gender model that situates 'mum' and 'Mario' in opposition to one another. In this scheme he has (biologically) inherited his mother's snobbishness but cannot accrue her feminine gendered knowledge, skills and approaches. However, he also locates his intentionality and, like Pete (see Chapter 2), suggests his constructed identity conceals laziness. The idea that certain domestic areas, sensory experiences, objects and practices, are incomprehensible, mystical, and even supernatural was expressed by English and Spanish men and often referred to in terms of gender (see Chapter 6). Men who feel they lack housewife knowledge often refer to the unknown and powerful. I also interviewed women who told me that they had no expert knowledge of housework. Like these men, they invested housewifely knowledge in other women, deferring to women with greater experience of housework. In contrast to men, they tended to use narratives of respect rather that mystification to refer to such expertise.

Like Spanish women informants, English women described traditional housewives as obsessive. Each of them related a vision of a housewife who transgressed the limits of a natural interest in housework. Several saw obsession with housework as a problem, suggesting that people who spend too much time cleaning and/or thinking about cleaning must have something missing in their lives. Jane used her aunt as an example.

> I mean my mum's sister is just obsessive. We were talking about it just yesterday. She's got tiles in a few of the sort of living rooms in the house. And she basically washes the floors every day I think and she has this list of things to do every day and apparently she said to mum, 'Oh yes but I don't actually pull the fridge out and the cooker and stuff like that every day – I'll probably only do that probably once or twice a week.' And I mean she is absolutely obsessed. The minute you put a teaspoon down on the surface in the kitchen, it would be gone. And I just can't be like that . . . you know I think it's sad that someone gets like that. I think there must be something missing in their lives, to me, to have to be like that.

Jane's objection was not to her aunt's gender role, but to her interpretation of it: Jane was happy to live out a gendered division of labour when she was married herself, but characterized her own housework as enjoyable because, unlike her aunt, she did it when she was 'in the mood for it': 'I don't want to just do it because I've got to do it sort of thing. I'm not going to do it for the sake of it.'

One retired informant told me that she saw a lack in the lives of people who are too concerned with cleaning:

> *Informant:* I think there are more important things in life and it's something that has to be done but it's something you should get through as quickly as you can and as efficiently as you can and the best way to do it is quickly and efficiently.
> *Sarah:* And do you think it's a problem when people get obsessive about it?
> *Informant:* I think there's something wrong, there must be something very wrong with their lives if they think a lot about cleaning.
> *Sarah:* Yes, what do you think's missing?
> *Informant:* Interest. Fun.

However, for Maureen ,who described herself as 'houseproud' and 'really a home maker', the housework and gardening were central to her life. For her, cleaning her home was a part of enjoying her home:

> *Sarah:* And when you say you enjoy your home, what do you mean exactly?
>
> *Maureen:* Well, I just like keeping it nice and tidy. I mean I can't leave it or anything like that not when those are saying just leave it. I really enjoy, well I enjoy the cleaning part of it as well, you know.

Whilst for some this woman's approach would be obsessive, she was also able to refer to an example of 'fanatical' behaviour in relation to which she could define her own as reasonable:

> Well, funny enough, our niece was saying that her mother, she said, at one time in her life it was just unbearable because she just cleaned, cleaned, cleaned. And they had to clean as children, you know. Before they went to school they had to clean out cupboards and do the cutlery drawer. Well I think that's going over the score, you know.

The Housewife's Husband

Men and women non-housewife informants used the housewife and her expertise as contrast when representing their own identities. As their departures were from traditional gender as much as traditional femininity, the housewife's husband was also implicated. Here, as background to chapters 6 and 7, I explore him in terms of the gender relationships associated with housewife identities. The 'good partnership' of gender role segregation was the predominant relationship described by housewife informants. In England housewives mainly said their husbands were generally unskilled at and infrequently involved in housework, and some joked that their husbands were unable to do more than one thing at once: 'If my husband came down to the kitchen before me in the morning he would stand and watch the kettle boil. If it is me who is down first I will have put the washing machine on and started to make to toast while I'm waiting for it boil.' However, women were not necessarily critical of their husband's domestic roles. For example one retired couple spoke of their happy collaboration as a team.

> *Wife:* I think between us we have a pretty good partnership.
>
> *Husband:* You do all the cleaning and I do the maintenance.
>
> *Wife:* You do the maintenance.
>
> *Husband:* I do the decorating, the repairing.
>
> *Wife:* The outside painting.
>
> *Husband:* Woodwork, etc.
>
> *Wife:* If anything falls off – say a door handle falls off, he'll put it back on again.

These informants organized their homes through traditional gender role segregation. They fitted the material home into this division in interesting ways. For example in several cases women spoke of their relationship with their husbands in connection with laundry technologies. They described how they abused their technologies by overloading the washing machine or by causing a potential fire hazard by failing to clean the filter in the tumble dryer or not timing the dryer. In doing so they referred to their husbands as the protectors of these technologies, and the regulators of their use of them. Whilst their husbands would not engage with housewifely knowledge about housework, they would not engage with technical knowledge, and neither would they take responsibility for applying this knowledge to the practical use of the domestic machinery at their disposal, even though they were aware that by doing so they created fire hazards and risked breakages.

Several women saw their partner's role as one of 'helping', often constructing a husband as well meaning but not competent. For example, a Spanish informant who saw herself as a housewife told me her husband prepared some of his own meals and occasionally washed up, made their bed, or mopped the floor. However, he did not usually perform these tasks to her standards.

Informant: Yes, when he's here in the morning he says, I mopped up for you, and I say, OK.
Sarah: And does he do it?
Informant: Yes, and then I come and do it again.
Sarah: Does he know that you do that?
Informant: No.

Likewise, an English housewife, described her experiences when her husband, who had retired a few months before she was due to retire from her full-time job, offered to take responsibility for the housework during this period. He did the housework but she did it again after him:

Sarah: Did he not do it at all or did he just not do it well enough?
Informant: Well, he didn't do it well enough. I mean he'd clean the sink but he didn't do it well enough for me. The bathroom, he would wash the sink maybe but nothing else. The bath was never properly washed – not well enough for me anyway. I mean he might have done it but he just ran over it with a coaster thing. So I suppose it wasn't done to my, I didn't let him know that, of course.
Sarah: Right, so you didn't say anything.
Informant: Didn't say anything, no. I had to be very, very careful cos it's always like, he was doing his best with it, and I mean he could

have been spending the first months of his retirement doing other things, so I was grateful. And of course he made the food or something, you know, when I came in, so that was a big thing wasn't it?

Similarly of the nine women who told me that their husbands pegged out their laundry badly, only one had told him she was unhappy with the standard of his work. The housewives I spoke with had a great monopoly of knowledge that served them well in their dealings with the husbands and sons who Morley would have *them* serve. These men knew only what the housewife decided to reveal about the practices and processes of domestic life. Sometimes strategies of deceit were embedded in the power relations of family life. They depended on strategic use of sensory knowledge that housewives, but not their husbands or children, had access to. Alice described how if she found her son's jeans on the floor and she does not consider them to be sufficiently dirty to wash, she would return them to his wardrobe as if clean:

I say to him oh I'm not washing them yet but sometimes he'll chuck them on the floor to be washed so if they're really screwed up I just pick them up and put them on a hanger and I'll put them back in his wardrobe. *So he thinks I've washed them.* I haven't but I think jeans you can wear you know three or four times easily.

Conclusion: Housewives and the Home

The traditional housewife and her knowledge are critiqued, abused, elevated to the supernatural, and lived out as the everyday gendered experience of many contemporary women. As my informants' examples show, there are many ways of being a housewife, both in Spain and England, and this might not mean living up to the ideal. Women's relationships to the home are both diverse and changing in Spain and England. This does not mean that the housewife will disappear, but that she must be resituated, both in terms of how anthropology places her theoretically and as way of understanding how and why she might be important in the lives of others.

Similar themes of the use of and need for housewifely knowledge, the mystical quality of housewifely power to clean and resolve domestic problems and the empty life of the obsessive housewife, were part of the worlds of both English and Spanish non-housewife informants. In discussions with these informants, the housewife, in Spain and England, is in a risky position: she may be obsessive and verging on madness, and her life is incomplete, empty or imbalanced if she thinks about housework too much. As such, she is used as a means of constructing difference amongst women, by women who insist that their lives should be different. These discussions situate the housewife symbolically quite differently from the way Morley and McHugh suggest. She is indeed in danger, but not so much of becoming unclean through her everyday contact with dirt, as of losing control of her search for meaning in her life by overindulging in the constant routine of housework. By using notions of madness and obsession my informants echoed the works reviewed above that emphasize the importance of 'getting out of the home' and call for housewives to become more fulfilled by developing their interests outside the home, as a means of preventing isolation and depression. Although my informants did not see overindulgence in housework as a sign of depression, they considered it to be an obsession that could both cause and reveal unfulfilled lives. By making a focus on housework into a metaphor for obsessive behaviour and madness my informants were arguing for a femininity that rejects traditional gender. For them, an over-commitment to domestic routine constituted a transgression. In doing so they excluded the femininity of the 'good housewife' from the mainstream, situating it as a marginalized, mad feminine identity. The traditional housewife lived in a world of different values, priorities and sensory knowledge and practices from those of most of my informants, and yet they still needed her, and depended on her expertise. They dealt with this in various ways – by elevating her to having supernatural 'mum power', or, by making her obsessive, placing her at the edge of sanity. With the exceptions discussed above, most of the housewives I interviewed did not represent themselves as a 'good housewife', but as normal women who cut corners in their housework, had happy fulfilled lives, and whose priorities lay elsewhere. However, housewives themselves are not all the same: just as we need to attend to diversity within gender categories, it is unrealistic to expect all housewives to constitute their identities in the same way in their different homes and families. Some of my informants lived out their preferred identities through domestic routine and fulfilment, others were proud to describe their everyday gender performativity to indicate they were not ideal housewives. Each interpreted the housewife role according to her own script and priorities. The housewife not only has the autonomy that Oakley endowed her with to organize her own day, she can also choose what sort of housewife she will be.

My informants' descriptions of the housewife also situated her in relation to her material home quite differently from the feminist approaches that would have her imprisoned and lonely in the labyrinth of masculine architectural structures. Instead they emphasized her expert and privileged knowledge and the power this endowed her with. The housewives I described above imposed their own values on lacy knickers and crumpled jeans. *They* used their sensory knowledge and the morality that this implied to determine whether material objects had sufficiently smooth textures, smelt clean, or looked clean. Their relationships with these material objects situated them in relation to other people in their homes.

In this chapter I have indicated some of the ways in which Spanish and English men and women have situated the housewife as a gendered cultural icon. In giving meaning to the housewife, her knowledge and practices, they simultaneously implicate their own identities, and inevitably, through their own housework and home decoration practices, not only constitute their own identities, but do so in terms of their personal departures from what they see as tradition. The following two chapters take this up to explore, through a series of case studies, how different Spanish and English men and women negotiate their gendered identities in their sensory homes.

6

Departing from Obsession: Femininities at Home

English and Spanish women are living out new and diverse roles, and giving increasing value to, amongst other things, education, training, career and travelling. Statistical sources cited in Chapter 1 show they are having fewer children and, although they still do more housework than men, they are doing less than they were. Many are also intentionally rejecting characteristics, practices and sets of knowledge that they associate with the housewife role. Ethnographic studies have demonstrated that women are not simply passive domestic servants in systems of patriarchy. Rather women's roles in creating and maintaining their homes can signify relationships of equality with, rather than of oppression by, their partners (e.g. Gullestad 1993, Silva 2000). These developments are interrelated with those in the public sphere. For example Borrell (1992) has explored the progress of Spanish women's entry into the public sphere including adult education, and Alberdi's quantitative work shows how Spanish women have come to devalue domestic work in favour of salaried work outside the home (1999: 229–65). As I have shown in *Women and Bullfighting* (Pink 1997a), Spanish women actively participate in new ways in traditional activities that had previously been almost exclusively masculine. The bullfight provides a good example of how as such women are engaging with sensory embodied knowledge and practices that had hitherto been seen as masculine. Such women do not necessarily live in nuclear family contexts – there has been a rise in people living alone, along with a decreasing birth rate and an increasing divorce rate. However, those studies that look at working women's lives at home usually focus on their home lives in terms of how domestic work is negotiated with their male partners and children. Often this is couched as the problem of women working a double shift (e.g. Alberdi 1999: 238) and the resolution of this when men begin to take equal responsibility for domestic work. Sociological studies of English women's experiences of domestic life reflect similar themes of family and the couple (e.g. Sullivan 2000). Such studies inform my analysis here but this research departs from existing work on women's roles and identities in couples and families by exploring how women in other situations live out and express their gendered identities at home, including women living alone or in flat shares, widowed and divorced women and single mothers. In this chapter I discuss how women who are not housewives, and who do not necessarily live with a male partner, perform their feminine identities in their sensory homes. This means a focus on how they prioritize *their* values, how they situate themselves in relation to traditional gender, the discourses they refer to in constructing their femininities, and their relationships with the practices of housework and decoration, and with sensory elements of and spatial design of their homes. I shall examine how housework and home creativity are processes through which different sorts of feminine identities are constituted.

Women who do their own housework and home decoration are engaging with activities that have for the most part (apart from some aspects of home decoration in England) been gendered feminine and have been associated with an everyday traditional housewifely femininity. Nevertheless each woman's identity is complex, her femininity is constituted uniquely, and being a woman does not exclude also having some components of one's identity that are traditionally masculine or involve one engaging in masculine activities. This is particularly evident for women working in mainstream 'masculine' occupations. As McElhinny (1994) shows, in the US, women police officers 'interpret behaviour that is normally and frequently understood as masculine (such as lack of emotionality or displays of physical violence) as occupational' (Cornwall and Lindisfarne 1994a: 7) and 'repeatedly engage in *both* stereotypically "masculine" and "feminine" activities' (Cornwall and Lindisfarne 1994b: 17). In Spain women bullfighters similarly engage in sets of behaviour that are associated with both traditional masculinity and femininity (Pink 1997a). Likewise women who are not housewives sometimes engage in 'traditionally' masculine tasks at home, in addition to undertaking tasks that are associated with traditional femininity.

Rejecting the Housewife Role: Domestic Knowledge, Organization and Routine

Women who do not consider themselves housewives accumulate and employ a limited amount of knowledge about housework. Rather than engaging with the values and sensory knowledge that inform the processes by which housewives undertake their duties, my informants preferred to apply their own theories and moralities to housework, its purpose and frequency. When necessary they referred to respected expert housewife relatives or friends, however they were interested in applying this expertise to develop a process, rather than fully working through the sensory knowledge and the moral values to which it is attached.

Spanish and English women shared some approaches and points of departure from what they saw as tradition, although they referred to culturally specific values and knowledge. My informants' notions of domestic routine provide an example. Whereas all my Spanish informants told me that routine played a key role in their domestic organization, in England liberation from routine was seen as fundamental to being the independent person that so many of my informants represented themselves as. Correspondingly English informants linked everyday housework routines almost exclusively to the lifestyle of a housewife. In contrast, in Spain Pilar, a teacher, valued her free time and did not clean daily. Although she felt housework should not be prioritized she believed there should be 'balance' between different areas of life, seeing keeping a clean home as part of that. To maintain her active working, cultural and social life and keep a clean home, she consciously maintained a routine by employing a cleaner with whom she collaborated in housework. In general Spanish women said they could achieve an appropriate balance in their lives through an organized housework routine. For non-housewives, if affordable, this was likely to incorporate the paid work of a cleaner. In contrast, rather than employing a cleaner, whose weekly visits they felt might impose a routine on *them*, English informants said they incorporated cleaning into their own emotional and expressive narratives at home. They did housework when they were in the mood and as such found it therapeutic. For example Jane and Nicola, both 'independent' women, said the only routines they followed were dictated by their jobs outside the home. They didn't mind cleaning as long as they could do it when they felt inclined; 'when you've got the bug' as Nicola put it or as Jane described as part of a personal narrative:

> You suddenly feel like you want a clear out or something. Or you want to clean up and that's when I do it. I don't do it regularly. I don't think I have to do it and if I don't feel like doing it then I don't do it. I certainly don't do my washing up in a morning. I just let it pile up until I think, oh I'll do the washing up now.

This ensured that for them housework would not be experienced as it was described by Oakley's informants as repetitive and compared to 'the emotionally frustrating sense of being on a treadmill that requires the same action to be repeated again and again' (1985: 46). Oakley's housewife informants also claimed that 'cleaning is only a bore when one's mood is out of tune with it: conversely, in the "right" mood, cleaning is cheerfully and quickly done' (Oakley 1985: 53). In contrast to my non-housewife informants, who did not clean unless they were in the mood, for Oakley's housewives being in the 'wrong mood' was a negative aspect of housework (1985: 59) and was one of the things that make it unenjoyable. Thus, for Spanish non-housewives, having a balance in their lives included cleanliness in their home and was objectified in the form of routine. For English non-housewives, the right balance in one's life was objectified by independently following one's own natural emotional and personal narrative, into which a clean home might be incorporated as and when this narrative allowed. The importance of following one's natural disposition is illustrated in the case of Christine, who considered herself 'undomesticated' and practised minimal and sporadic housework but organized her care of her horses in ways that paralleled traditional housewifery. Christine was in her late fifties, and had retired from an office job to a country cottage with land and stables for her horses. She had a clear sense of herself and her priorities:

> I'm talkative. And a very strong person I'd say and a good worker, at things I like doing. I do a lot of work with my horses. I prefer to work outside. I wouldn't say I'm very domesticated. I have someone to do my housework and I like going out socially, for meals in pubs, and I like a good book, a good film and I don't do any other sport seriously apart from riding, because obviously that takes a lot of time up.

This was consistent with Christine's description of her everyday life: she got up at half-past seven, fed her horses and dogs and then had her own breakfast before riding or turning out the horses and walking the dogs. After mucking out the stables with a friend's help, she would look after the land, pick up horse droppings, work in the fields, or garden, all, she noted, forms of outdoor work. She would have a light lunch, which would be followed by more outdoor work, dog walking, and horse care. At about half-past seven she would be ready for her evening meal. Christine was 'out three nights out of seven' and had friends over for meals or drinks on other evenings. She did not cook every night, and when she did she would make a meal that would last for two evenings. An important aspect of Christine's lifestyle was her autonomy. Like the housewives of Oakley's (1985) study (see Chapter 5), Christine compared her daily life with salaried work, in that 'I have got responsibilities but no actual boss over me seeing that I'm doing everything on time and things like that.' However, Christine did not spend her days doing housework. As Christine emphasized, she worked hard:

I'm a woman and a lot of people couldn't do what I do . . . There is quite a lot of heavy work to do. And I think most women who like horses could muck out but then that horsey people are that sort of people usually, they're outdoor people. But probably a person who's more interested in house things would find it very physically difficult.

Running her stables, like housework, gave no financial reward, and, like caring for a home, involved cleaning, routine, monotonous and physical tasks, often performed alone. However, for Christine, this work was not 'boring', but a means of living her 'horsey' outdoor self. Her dislike for housework was connected to her personal preferences and identity choices. Christine felt she had 'always' been an outdoor person, noting her childhood preference for gardening over housework. As she pointed out, 'some people like housework and some don't and I hate housework. I suppose that there again it's a love of the horses.' Christine now employed a cleaner two hours a week, who did 'mundane' housework tasks, and whilst she would not like guests to 'come in and find it awful' she was not 'houseproud' and believed 'a home is to be lived in'.

Although not in Christine's case, in England the notion of laziness as a personal quality was mentioned frequently by my informants. Virginia who had, to my mind, not been at all lazy in the way she had beautifully decorated her new rented home, by repainting it, displaying ornaments and hanging pictures, felt she was lazy. Several informants explained their failure to wash up or do basic chores in terms of laziness and noted that a key motivation for overcoming this and 'making themselves' do some housework would be if they were expecting a visitor. Others spoke of their attitude to home decoration in terms of laziness. Jenny, whose house was tastefully and thoughtfully decorated, felt that it was her laziness that prevented her from taking her home decoration a step further: 'Not really, you can see the sort of . . . I have to really do this, I want to do this room, actually. I'd like to do it a sort of goldy colour. But I'm so lazy.' Jenny said she would rather spend her time and money on travelling than on home decorating, but, like my informants who felt they had a lazy attitude to housework, she took a moral perspective on this that saw being a good homemaker as a proper traditionally moral activity that she was not prepared to live up to. Thus Jenny and other informants rejected traditional values that associate women with home (as cleaners and decorators), through statements that spoke of their independence, narratives of free choice and love of travel and the public rather than the domestic. Whilst personal narratives of emotions and personality structured the everyday for English informants, for Spanish informants the question of laziness did not arise since a conscious routine and maintaining the balance, with or without the help of a cleaner, structured their everyday. Rather than seeing themselves as lazy, Spanish non-housewife women informants took a different perspective. Most made it clear they had far better things to do with their lives than constant housework, emphasizing their professional lives, love of travel and of socializing in public space. In doing so, like my English informants, they were identifying themselves with activities that are traditionally associated with masculine social space and narratives of travel and exploration.

Women as Homemakers

As homemakers, women are creative and imaginative agents in wider processes of change. Other work on England supports this view. Silva has rightly critiqued the idea that women are necessarily dominated by men or used as 'assets' by families (Silva 2000: 24–5) and has argued that through their domestic consumption practices women are active and strategic agents. Likewise Clarke challenges the idea that home decoration and consumption are simply expressive or normative practices. She shows how her women informants living in standardized council housing 'appropriate, interpret and generate agency through their standardized spaces' (Clarke 2001: 29). This is of course not an exclusively British practice. Garvey describes how in Norway a single woman informant living alone unconventionally painted her post box, window frames and house name plate white, rather than having the decorative motifs and name plates traditionally exhibited in her neighbourhood. Garvey interprets this as her informants' way of positioning herself socially 'as a key player in a certain subversive relationship with her perception of popular social values' (2001: 64).

The roles ordinary contemporary women play in home decoration involve a series of activities that are gendered feminine and masculine, and that vary cross-culturally. For instance in Spain and England traditional gendering of home decoration is different. 'Do it yourself' (DIY) and home maintenance in England have been seen as masculine tasks, involving painting and decorating, amateur carpentry and power tools and visits to DIY stores. In this model, as my informants discussed it, men drill and paint while women vacuum up the sawdust and launder their overalls. In contrast in Southern Spain the traditional annual whitewashing of the inside (and in some cases outside) of the home is part of the job of a housewife. In fact, although traditional models persist, many contemporary women are responsible for the embodied labour of home decoration and improvement as well as home design, and the acquisition and manipulation of the materials and objects required. In doing so, they articulate their agency as well as their aspirations in a process from which emerge both self and home. For example Silva (2000) discusses the domestic consumption practices of three women, two of whom live with their husbands and children and work part-time and one unemployed single mother. Suggesting that practices 'expressing particular senses of social inclusion or exclusion' have been especially relevant for women, Silva shows how the material culture and technologies these women have acquired and selected for their homes are linked with their 'specific strategies of advancement in social space', thus arguing that women are active agents who through careful consumption are capable of taking the family into 'a more valued social space' (2000: 24). Clarke similarly represents her informants as creative individuals. She argues that through the decoration of their homes, that in fact are rarely seen by others, these women objectify 'the vision the occupants have of themselves in the eyes of others' and thus their decorated homes become 'an entity and process to live up to, give time to and show off to' (Clarke 2001: 42). In both these studies, women's relationships to their visual decoration are seen as complex and interwoven with their aspirations and the projects they have for themselves and their families. This connection between imagination, aspirations, creativity and the material home is at the basis of my discussion here. Miller (2001b) suggests houses are 'haunted' by the agency of past occupants, the council, and architectural design, and that people take possession of their homes through home decoration as a form of objectification of the self *vis-à-vis* the material culture of home. Broadly in agreement with this idea, I extend it to examine how my informants' possession of their homes might also be transient and was articulated through their representations of sensory embodied experience and strategies.

Existing work emphasizes the material visual/visible aspects of home decoration, but neglects the embodied experience of home decoration revealed by my research. For example Christine's intention was to create a 'dream' home. She and her husband had their cottage altered extensively, adding rooms and bathrooms and moving the front door. They had re-thatched the roof and created the garden. Nonetheless Christine had further plans: 'my next project would be, I'd like to get a tiled roof on the garage. I feel that's not in keeping with the rest of the house.' When they bought the cottage it was in a bad state. Christine had detailed memories, having made home decoration part of her everyday life for several years:

This hallway here I decorated on my own. It was terrible, I mean there was holes. I had to wallpaper even the ceiling. I had to really, it was a just a mess in here, completely. It took me like all winter just working afternoons, but it does look a lot better now I think. Right, and these are the new stairs and I decorated all this myself with wallpaper. I had to have scaffolding up here and this sort of took me two or three winters to do.

In Christine's example we can see how the performance of her identity as a strong and determined woman, capable of physical work, was facilitated by the challenges presented in her home decoration project. Christine worked on and papered 'difficult' walls and it was with these walls and the materials and tools that she used to work on them that her home and sense of self emerged. The difficult walls facilitated her manifestations of her strength and her taste. In her descriptions of this work Christine emphasized that she had chosen which sort of activity she was prepared to invest her own embodied labour in. Other women make other choices.

Smell, also neglected in the existing literature, is key to how women described their departures from or ascriptions to housewifely femininity. In the Prologue I described how Maureen's olfactory home creativity involving products, sprays, oils, candles, and perfumes was expressive of her homemaker identity. At the same time, without the olfactory properties of the home she lived in, the performativity through which she expressed herself would not have come into being. Likewise in Chapter 5 I described how smell was part of Lola, enjoyable experience of cleaning in her bathroom. In a way that was embedded in her lifestyle, priorities and own expert knowledge, Christine also thought of her home as an olfactory space. Smell was an important part of Christine's world, and she was careful to ensure that neither herself nor her home smelt of horses. Like other informants, she liked her home to look and smell clean, and she noted that after her cleaner's visits 'I come in and say that smells lovely and clean.' As far as Christine was concerned, in general houses posed greater health risks than her stables. Moreover, she noted, 'alright people don't like the smell of manure heaps but to me that's a country smell and . . . dirty drains and things like that is a lot worse smell to me'. Christine saw her home and her stables as two distinct olfactory worlds that she could assess in terms of particular olfactory cues related to indoors and outdoors, the domestic and the countryside. Other women informants, purposefully rejecting a housewifely routine, noted that they would clean their kitchen sinks when they noticed that vegetables trapped under the washing up bowl had already or could potentially become smelly, or they would not leave dirty pots for so long that they could get smelly. Thus they framed their control of domestic odours with a clean but not obsessive or routine approach, and based it on their personal experiences and 'natural' responses to bad smells rather than on housewifely knowledge.

In Chapter 4 I introduced the idea of sound as an important element of home. As Tacchi (1998) has shown, people use radio both to create part of the texture of home and in the construction of self. Music and radio were also implicated in my informants' homemaking and performativity (see Chapter 4). In the case I describe here music can be seen as part of the process of creating a sentiment of home (outlined in Chapter 3) rather than home as a physical space, and as something that is temporary rather than fixed. Holly shared her cousin's one-bedroom London flat. She slept on a sofa bed in the living room and her bed linen was kept in a cupboard. In the living room, Holly's identity, possessions and use of the space were intertwined with her cousin's homemaking. Holly had some of her own CDs and videos mixed in with those belonging to her cousin, and since they shared relatives there were photographs of some of her own family on display. She shared a wardrobe and space for cosmetics and perfume in her cousin's bedroom. Holly did not formally engage in home creativity, but followed her cousin's lead in continuing the processes needed for its maintenance. In fact Holly had her own vision of how she would like her home to be:

Holly: If it was my kitchen? If I had the money . . . sort of futuristic and everything, I think. Be all silver and metal and glass all over the place.

Sarah: Yes, why's that?

Holly: Cos I just sort of like, I don't know, modern and trying to be really modern and if I had the money I mean I would do it, by all means. You sort of see places on, people's houses on, you know, American shows and things, and films, and you just see massive studios and they all look really nice, and you know. Or I'd just have it all like seventies colours, you know, all mad and wild and like all swirls and things all over the place and that's what I love. Because that's my personality, that's, you know, that'd be bringing it out.

However, in reality Holly only visually mapped her social identity in the flat by using magnets to stick a photo of her godson on the side of the fridge. This contrasted with her cousin's more formal displays of framed family photographs and ornaments. A visual survey of the flat might lead one to assume that Holly had no personal space. Nonetheless the way the flat was shared could not simply be understood in terms of spatial and visible elements. The uses and meanings of space and place were not fixed but varied and changed throughout each day. When I asked Holly if sharing space in the flat with her cousin was a problem, she explained that in a sense they each had their own space:

We don't, you know, bump into each other because we go at different times. She goes at eight o'clock in the morning, I go at half eleven in the morning, so we miss each other. You know it's not a fight to get in the shower or anything. We have our space . . . we do see each other a lot but I'm always out or she's like working late or she's gone out, maybe gone out for a drink with some work mates or something. But yes, we don't get in each other's way.

It was within her own temporal space at home that Holly could be 'at home'. Although she had done little to create the visual home, she created her own domestic soundscapes, with TV and music, and an olfactory world. Because she started work at twelve noon, most of Holly's time at home was in the morning. From the moment she got up, she set about creating and enacting her home and identity, being herself:

> I get up about half eight – as soon as I get up I stick music on, which consists of Aretha Franklin, Guns n' Roses, everything. If the kitchen's a mess, I'll just tidy it up. You know, watch TV for a bit but basically sing, dance all over the place, get ready for work and I'm normally fine . . . You see I've got time to myself then and stick on music, that gets me going. Sort of lifts me up in the morning.

Holly created herself and her home within an architectural space but employed time and sound in doing so, using very limited visual self-expression. To do so she reorganized her domestic soundscape, perhaps each morning in a slightly different way. Drawing from a study of how her Norwegian informants periodically reorganize their furniture, Garvey has suggested that this involves a voluntary process of emotional renewal. Holly's temporary rearrangement of her domestic soundscape according to her own tastes has parallels with the material practices of Garvey's informants. It provides a way of changing her cousin's organization of the home, and thus of taking possession of the home that, unlike the project she described for the kitchen, is easily reversible.

In making homes in England and Spain women are creative, imaginative agents who work with a variety of material, sensory, social and emotional resources to create expressive spaces that are the outcome of negotiations between these multiple agencies. How can we view these womens' departures from traditional gender as constituted in their housework and home decoration as an index through which changing gender in Spain and England might be discussed?

Agency, Performativity and the Sensory Home

Above I have shown how different women have demonstrated and spoken about (i.e. *represented* in their interviews with me) their practices of housework and home decoration, and suggested that they have self-consciously resisted or departed from what they perceive as a traditional domestic femininity. Their agency has been explicit and intentional even though it is not necessarily thought out in each of their actions. Nevertheless, as I have noted in Chapters 3 and 4, it would be unwise to see this agency as unfettered. Clearly economic and class differences impact on the freedom my informants have to do as they would like. However, recognizing this, it is not my intention to relate their ability to participate as agents of changing gender with their economic situations. Indeed Christine, who had retired to a more affluent lifestyle and could now employ a cleaner, described how even when she worked full-time her everyday performativity resisted the values and housework practices she associated with a housewifely approach. Like other informants, she had cleaned 'quickly' in preparation for dinner parties and other events rather than as a matter of routine. Moreover, as Clarke's (2001) comparison of the home creativity of middle and working-class women implies, women with lower incomes do not necessarily have less agency and creativity. Rather they employ these attributes to acquire and work with resources and materials in different ways.

Women's agency intersects with the social, material and sensory contexts of home. Agency is not solely human but of the buildings and the objects as well. It has been suggested that women might become both oppressed and depressed by the patriarchal discourses that are embedded in the architectural design of flats and houses as well as moral discourses about womens' 'proper' roles (see Chapter 5). This was not the case for most of my women informants. Instead, many contemporary women's practices are both critical of and resist traditional gender and conventional domestic layouts and uses of space. As such their interactions with their material and sensory homes constitute forms of changing gender and changing homes by giving new meanings or layouts to areas of the home and to the activities carried out in it. In England Christine followed a conventional domestic layout, but unconventionally used her kitchen for chatting and having coffee with friends, rather than for cooking and cleaning. Holly's projects of home and identity came together in temporary spaces created with music, television and her embodied actions, where she performed not housewifely tasks but relaxed and prepared herself to go out to work for the day. In each of these cases, as I have outlined above, my informants negotiated with different social, material and sensory agencies of home. Through these everyday practices and forms of organization, both homes and genders that depart from what my informants perceived as traditional housewifery and home came into being.

Departures from Tradition, New Moralities and Understandings of Change and Difference

My non-housewife informants engaged with both housework and home-making, although to different degrees and on different terms. Although they regarded both activities as potential outlets for their self-expression, in general they embraced homemaking with considerably more enthusiasm than housework. Whereas they saw their housework practices as departures from negative housewifely approaches they represented home-making not so much as an activity that was associated with a femininity they did not ascribe to but as part of a personal project that would be expressive of their own taste and identity. As such they defined their own approaches to housework and home creativity as being in some way natural to themselves as individuals. My English women informants tended to define traditional housewifely femininity as 'obsessive' and sought mainly to depart from this in terms of the way they situated housework in relation to other priorities and activities. In particular this meant not being a slave to routine, but instead making housework into an activity that was responsive to other more natural narratives that they felt were important elements of their identities and informed their sense of self. They would do housework when they felt like it, 'when I've got the bug' as Nicola put it. As far as they were concerned, this was the only time housework would be enjoyable, and could in fact be therapeutic, and thus complementary to the everyday spontaneity of the emotional narratives they prioritized. Importantly these women were not prepared to compromise what they saw as their own natural identity – or, in other words, their sense of self – by conforming to the demands of housewifery. Although in terms of their work outside the home most of them were active and committed, in their relation to domestic work these women constructed themselves as lazy, with an interest in things not of the house, and independent. By attributing these characteristics to themselves as natural or innate, they subsequently constructed the obsessive housewife as unnatural. However, in making connections between their self-identities and their housework practices, these women informants were also often ironic and reflexive. Indeed, whilst criticizing the housewife on the one hand, they simultaneously recognized the importance of her knowledge as a respected resource that they might refer to. However, they were also careful not to engage with the processes by which this knowledge might be produced themselves, and instead expected to be able to ask expert housewives for instructions that would solve a housework problem, rather than for knowledge that would inform their own resolution of the problem.

Thus these women informants constructed their relationships with their material and sensory homes in ways that they felt were not housewifely. Their home creativity and interactions with their material and sensory environments, entailed what we might see as self-conscious homemaking linked with their articulation of their conscious projects of self-identity and of home. The homes and identities that come into being through this intersubjectivity between the individual and her environment will be the outcome of the negotiations between human, material and sensory elements, rather than the imposition of an imprint on the environment by the individual. Nevertheless human agency and intentionality clearly show through as we consider how each woman went about responding to her environment and the identity statements she hoped to represent in doing so. Seeing their homes as sanctuaries (in which they could do as they liked and wear what they wanted), where external routines or norms need not apply, these women informants closely guarded both their autonomy and their privacy in their homes. They mapped their own priorities onto traditional layouts in ways that contested housewifely priorities – as I noted, Christine's kitchen was less for cooking than for chatting and most younger women informants had computers in their homes, kept in the living room or a study/spare bedroom. Holly created *her* home through music in her cousin's flat. These English women's home creativity was also expressive of their departures from housewifeliness. As homemakers, they negotiated with the multiple material and social agencies of their homes – involving for instance, landlords, odours, sounds, textures, and the character and layout of their homes – to create homes that they later interpreted as expressive of their identities.

For these women, their independence, having the right or natural balance in their lives, and the pursuit of their own priorities were thus bound up in the production of home and gender in specific ways. By comparing Spanish women informants' departures from understandings of traditional gender with those of English women informants, I shall suggest such departures are culturally specific. Like my English women informants, Spanish women tended to define the traditional housewife as obsessive, in both the frequency and detail with which she engaged in housework. They emphasized how they viewed the world and in particular the home from a different perspective to the housewife: she could notice dirt that they could not 'see'. Like my English informants, these Spanish women felt that the housewife had the wrong balance in her life, arguing that all areas of one's personal, domestic and professional life should be give equal priority as each complements and indeed depends on the others. Whilst my Spanish informants did not see their housewife contemporaries as slaves to routine, they did suggest that their everyday and weekly routines did not have enough variation, and were too centred on housework. They emphasized the importance of having other things in ones life, and in particular spoke of the importance of career and work, studying, travel, going out and having time to oneself (for example, to write poetry, relax at home alone, stare at the ceiling or go out for a walk) in their own lives. In contrast to my English informants, however, Spanish women did not depart from a housewifely identity by rejecting the idea of domestic routine. Indeed they emphasized the importance of routine in maintaining the balance that was essential to their lives. Each informant described to me how she would organize her housework on a weekly basis according to an established routine. Whilst on occasion she would miss or have to postpone a housework activity because something more important or interesting would tempt her away, the routine formed an important template that structured her relationship with her home. These routines also served to define the way in which informants interacted with their material and sensory homes. Informants tended to develop strategies that would ensure that routines were maintained, by enlisting the help of a cleaner or a relative if they were unable to complete the tasks themselves. For my English informants, housework was subject to their emotional narratives. In contrast, my Spanish informants seemed to view this relationship between the self and the home differently, by seeing their emotional well-being as partially contingent on the maintenance of a balance that was largely structured through the organization of everyday life. Their departures from housewifely practices referenced the routine of the housewife, but contested it: these informants engaged in routine to attend to the housework tasks that were required by someone who could not 'see' everything that the housewife would regard as dirt; and they took on paid help or other assistance to ensure the completion of housework whilst freeing them to 'get on with my life', as one informant put it.

Spanish women informants also departed from traditional femininity through their home creativity and use of space. Their bedrooms and living rooms were equipped with computers and doubled up as their studies, tasteless traditional ornaments belonging to landlords were hidden in the sideboard, and furniture was placed in rooms it was not conventionally intended for. Paintings, posters and objects brought home from travel abroad in Eastern Europe, Asia and Africa (hardly traditional Spanish holiday destinations) often decorated the walls of my informants' homes, contesting the traditional association of women with the domestic sphere, and stating that these informants had stepped out of it. As the creativity and priorities of these women were developed in negotiation with the physical and sensory environments, both home and gender emerged as departures from the embodied practices and spatial organization of traditional Spanish housewifery. The home creativity of the Spanish women and the English women discussed above can be interpreted as a form of resistance. However, their resistance forms a feminine critique of traditional feminine organization and decoration of the home, rather than an instance of binary feminine domesticity resisting the imposition of a masculine design.

As they lived out these critiques, departures, and contestation, of traditional femininity and the traditional home, these English and Spanish women also engaged in moral commentaries. In doing so, I suggest, they were asserting new moralities that depart from the moralities of traditional gender discourses. By naturalizing their own methods of domestic organization albeit in different ways (in England as responsive to their natural spontaneous emotional and personal narratives, and in Spain as essential to the natural balance in their lives that is required for a sense of well-being) and contrasting these to the traditional housewife, they were suggesting that for them to be a housewife would be unnatural. These statements are themselves bound up with sensory embodied experience and metaphor. When women speak about how they decide when to do the housework, they differentiate between their own abilities to perceive and interpret sensory knowledge about dirt and cleanliness and those of a housewife. My women informants who resisted the housewife model referred to dirt that a housewifely moral discourse would identify as present but that they personally could not see or smell. For them, the priority was the embodied therapeutic (English) or balanced (Spanish) outcome of the accomplishment of housework when performed according to their 'natural' needs.

7

Engaging with Domestic Discovery:
Masculinities at Home

Since the late 1980s a growing field of men's studies has developed in anthropology, sociology, cultural studies and queer studies, partially as a response to the focus on women that perpetuated gender studies through-out the 1970s and early 1980s. This focus on masculinities is also linked to changing approaches to understanding gender, identity and how these are constituted. Since the 1990s critiques of positivist and generalizing approaches to masculinity (e.g. Connell's (1995: 32–4) critique of Gilmore's (1990) *Manhood in the Making*) have informed contemporary understandings of masculinity as a complex, multiple and diverse category, 'a vexed term, variously inflected, multiply defined, not limited to straightforward descriptions of maleness' (Berger, Wallis and Watson 1995: 2). Rather than having universal characteristics masculinity is thus 'a complex and discursive category that cannot be seen as independent from that of other productive components of identity' (Berger, Wallis and Watson 1995: 2). Whilst recognizing that wider and political issues like race, ethnicity and sexuality are never distant from the personal, it is not my priority to explore these here; rather the 'other components' I focus on emerge from my informants' self-definitions and cultural resources.

Existing work on masculinities in England and Spain has developed within different approaches to the anthropology of gender. Elsewhere (Pink 1997a, c.f. Hart 1994, Cornwall and Lindisfarne 1994a, 1994b and Loizos 1992) I have criticized the objectifying representations of Spanish masculinity in the work of Pitt-Rivers (1963), Gilmore (1987) and Brandes (1981), to argue that although their work might describe a tradi-tional hegemonic masculinity it does portray how all contemporary ordi-nary men constitute and experience their masculinities in their everyday lives. As Connell has shown in his study of Australian masculinities, we need to think in terms of multiple masculinities, and to recognize the diversity that exists within the categories of masculinity we create for the sake of analysis or representation as 'Seen up close hegemonic and complicit masculinities are no more monolithic than are subordinated and marginalised masculinities' (1995: 181). Connell's historical approach to changing European and American masculinities, describes 'complex structures of gender relations in which dominant, subordinate and marginalised masculinities are in constant interaction, changing the conditions for each others' existence and transforming themselves as they do' (1995: 198). In Spain and England traditional masculinities are no longer always dominant in everyday domestic and working life (and their dominance may never have been as universal as has been asserted). Nonetheless they often live on in certain public representations. As I point out in my analysis of Spain's bullfighting culture, these public representations should not be confused with how gender comes into being through the performativity of everyday life (see Pink 1997a).

Statistically in Spain and Britain more men are becoming responsible for organising or contributing to housework. In this chapter I discuss how my male informants incorporated such traditionally feminine activities into their masculine identities, and simultaneously represented their masculinities through their embodied performativity, sensory knowledge about domestic tasks, and home creativity. These new domestic masculinities depart from what my informants perceived as the traditional masculinity of the housewife's husband. Nevertheless when men spoke of their domestic practices they sometimes adopted traditional masculine narratives. The few existing studies of men's domestic roles tend to focus on men in families or with a female partner. In contrast I focus mainly on men who live alone, in house or flat shares and as single fathers.

Househusbands and Masculine Narratives

Of the little existing work on men's approaches to housework, Beer's study of househusbands stands out. In the 1970s Beer researched 'the experiences of men who do housework as it is commonly defined – cooking, cleaning, childcare, shopping, laundry, and household maintenance' (1983: x). Beer (following Oakley (1974 [1985]) argues that '*Responsibility* is what makes a housewife, even though husbands may "help out"', thus defining men who do more that 'helping out' by taking responsibility for housework as 'househusbands' (original italics). Some of these do housework full-time, some share it and do it part-time (1983: xi). Beer sets his analysis of househusbands in an American culture and society of the 1970s where both men's and women's expectations of gender roles and their actual activities were changing with men increasingly participating in housework.

Beer found househusbands' and housewives' feelings about housework often coincided: 'Men's dislikes seem to resemble many of the dislikes regarding housework expressed by housewives [i.e. those reported by Oakley (1985)]. They include the objections that housework can be boring, tedious, and repetitive, and that it can produce problems in sched-uling caused by conflicting priorities in outside work, social life, and standards of cleanliness' (1983: 106). According to Beer, house husbands' likes were 'the feelings of accomplishment, the affinity for neatness, and a clean home' (1983: 106). Men liked the tangible results of housework: it offers 'concrete pleasures and immediate gratification' whereas men's paid work has an 'alienated routine', 'rigid scheduling, the exchange of work for wages, and a lack of creativity' (Beer 1983: 107). Furthermore, whilst housework changes men in some ways, 'no men reported becoming more feminine'. Instead Beer suggested the 'greatest single effect of the househusbanding experience was to reduce the impor-tance of work outside the home' (1983: 107). Indeed, he constructed men's housework as an essentially masculine experience. I shall return to this below.

The very notion of a househusband indicates assumptions about the gendered composition of households (which may well have been more applicable to both theoretical themes and empirical realities in the 1970s). But it does not account for the increasing number of men who live alone, many out of choice, or for the contemporary diversity of masculine ex-periences of housework. In a context of multiple masculinities each man's identity is complex and constituted in relation to his personal trajectory and projects. Different masculinities are constructed, lived and repre-sented uniquely in relation to the structural, spatial, material, visual, sensory and social elements of men's homes. Below I explore this through examples and themes to examine how in engaging in housework and home creativity my informants conformed to, resisted or acted in coun-terpoint to architectural structures, traditional domestic practices, routines and knowledge, and gender discourses.

Masculine Departures: Meticulous but not Obsessive

In Chapters 5 and 6 I outlined how women non-housewife informants signified their difference from their mothers by carefully avoiding taking an obsessive approach to housework. My men informants behaved in a similar way. For example, Paul, aged twenty-four, lived in a shared student house where the housework was in theory shared but he noted that a rota had rapidly 'fallen apart'. He did his 'fair share', which 'basically just amounts to washing my own pots really. It's very rarely the rest of the house gets cleaned.' He found it annoying when 'you want to do some cooking and there's no pots available because they've all been used and left on the side or whatever, and something's been left to the point that colourful growths will appear on it', but felt he had become 'numb' to the state of the house and had to compromise his own standards. Paul related his own values to his biography: 'I was kind of brought up in a very clean house. Mum was always a very clean person, obsessed with cleanliness to be honest. She always wanted things clean if people were coming round. Even if generally you looked at it and you'd think it seemed really clean, she'd see the dirt in it, basically. 'Paul had a clear set of priorities when organising his working days at home. Housework was not excluded, but was undertaken in relation to his career development narrative, which meant prioritizing things to do with his career, mainly studying and surviving economically. Housework would 'usually end up on the list somewhere' but was 'of the least priority' as he described: 'I think to myself I really must hoover the room, I really must dust, it's a mess but I usually get round to them last.' However, like the English women I described in Chapter 6, when I asked Paul what would motivate him to do housework he told me:

> either I get the chance, I get the time so I say it really must be done, it's in a bad state, I must get it done, or, . . . I intend to get some work done but if I'm hitting a particular problem, I don't know, with my reading or one of the things I want to do, then cleaning becomes one of those prioritized things. If I had essays to do or something, in my student days, yes the cleaning would get done.

Thus, he subordinated housework to the needs created by activities that he considered key to his wider projects and his natural impulses.

Simon, aged thirty-two, had recently moved to London to start a new job. He lived in a one-bedroom rented flat, but felt he would soon buy his own place. In London Simon's new social world was interesting and busy with many parties, nights out, concerts and sporting events as well as visits from friends. This world was mapped out visually on the notice board in his dining area where he pinned concert and sports tickets, post-cards and flyers for nightclubs. He spent little time at home, seeing his flat as somewhere to recharge one or two evenings a week. With this lifestyle Simon rarely ate at home, even having breakfast at work. If he cooked he would make enough for more than one meal but said he usually ate convenience food: 'I've sort of got more lazy since I've got here because I can maybe afford the convenience foods that I couldn't before. I don't have, you know, well I don't get the time really to cook.' Although Simon spent little time at home he was nevertheless committed to creating a clean and tidy home with the resources and comfort he needed, seeing himself as 'a bit of a home entertainments junkie'. With an on-digital wide-screen TV with a sports package, video player and tapes, play station and CD player and collection, being at home for him was also an audio-visual experience that involved physical interaction. When he moved into the flat it had not been clean enough and he used visual and tactile metaphors to describe how he had found and dealt with the kitchen:

> Blimey, the oven was a real state and I had to get some oven cleaner and clean that out. There's still a fair amount of grease on that but that is still, it's still on there . . . there's still bits of grease and fat on here – don't touch it, it's all sticky . . . the back wall here and I've never been able to get that off. The actual insides of the cupboards, the actual bases of the shelves had grease as well and actually there's still bits. I mean all the metal bits here – I need to do it again actually – had a layer of grease on it. The floor was pretty filthy. The sink – I mean everything that was left here, even, was dirty. Things like there was a washing up brush that had had it. I threw that away straight away.

This approach carried through into his everyday relationship with his home:

> no matter how tidy it is at the time I always put things away or make a bit of an effort. I like to think I'm a bit of a snob. Although I'm a single guy and I'm sure they don't have any qualms about, you know, they don't really expect me to do that sort of thing. But I'll do it for my own sake, for my own pride. I suppose I was brought up to be fairly tidy. It's just pride really in your own surroundings.

However, Simon made his priorities clear, telling me that 'I place more importance on my social life at the weekend than doing the chores', and fitted housework, usually involving completely cleaning the kitchen and bathroom into Saturday or Sunday daytime. To measure his own approach to housework Simon contrasted himself with both his parents. He described his mother's last visit to his flat as follows: 'Even though I said "look, you know, you're here for the weekend, just enjoy yourself. Just have a break. Don't do anything", she still, I got up a bit late and she'd already been up two hours. She'd already cleaned my kitchen and wiped the floors thoroughly, got rid of the lime scale from the sink.' In fact Simon's father did most of the housework when Simon was a child, and during his school holidays or after school Simon would help with the housework, washing up, dusting, hovering and cleaning the bathroom once a week. Simon interprets his own approach to housework in terms of both his upbringing, and the sort of person he is. For instance he personally hates ironing, but understands his approach to ironing in terms of his 'meticulous' identity:

> I'm quite a meticulous person with most things – especially my work – so that will apply when it comes to things like ironing. And that's probably why it takes me so long. You know, make sure the collar is nice and straight and flat, you know, especially that awkward bit behind the collar, that bit at the top of the back, you know. I spend time doing there. Yes, even though I hate it I know it's got to be done.

Simon is nevertheless careful not to be obsessive, and contrasts his approach to his father's, noting:

> *Simon:* When I was growing up I probably didn't have the same sense of cleanliness he did and he would say 'Oh you've got to do that again' or 'Go over it.' Or, you know, I wouldn't move things out the way, I'd probably go round them and he'd say, 'Oh no you should take everything up and give it a thorough dusting down'
> *Sarah:* And do you do that now or not?
> *Simon:* Occasionally, occasionally. I'll maybe sometimes still go round things. If I think nobody's going to see it or it's not that, or if something's not going to be moved for a long time, I'll just leave it. I'll go round it. And maybe next time I'll move it out and do it properly. I haven't completely gone all the way like my dad.

Indeed the remaining sticky residue of grease in Simon's kitchen, that he had not 'been able' to remove, can be interpreted as emblematic of his refusal to go 'all the way'.

Paul's and Simon's interviews share some common themes. Although it would be foolish to use these to generalize about all men, they do indicate that, like women, men who do their own housework might coin their departures from housewifely approaches (as performed by women or other men) in terms of not being obsessive – a term both used. When men do housework they inevitably engage in practices and activities that are traditionally labelled feminine, but do so in ways that they reconcile with their own identities, values and priorities. However, we should also keep in mind the question of what it is these informants feel they are departing from when they compare themselves with an obsessive relative or friend. In Simon's case his father was just as likely to be obsessive about housework as his mother. Moreover Simon was not the only one of my English informants who told me that their father had taken principal responsibility for the housework. Virginia, for instance, told me that her father had been retired from military service. She described how her mother insisted that doing housework was expressive of her father's military character, implying that the housework was thus conceived through an ordered and meticulous masculine military narrative. Beer's study of househusbands was carried out in the 1970s, the decade when Virginia, Simon and my other informants of their generation were growing up. Not surprisingly, not all my men informants had grown up in worlds where only women did housework. Their departures might be seen as being from both the house-wife and her husband. However, they similarly sought to distance them-selves from obsessive masculine approaches to housework.

Above I introduced the idea of 'meticulous' identities. In Spain men informants also constructed continuities between their sense of self and housework, representing their housework as expressive of the sort of man they felt they were. Manolo, a retired man living alone, is meticulous, and committed to a daily cleaning routine, although he employs a cleaner:

> I like the way I have things, and if someone comes and disrupts that, I can't stand it . . . I can't stand dirt. For example, you see those portraits? The way they're hanging? I like them always to be like that. The woman comes, she moves things around when she's cleaning, and I tell her: 'No, that's got to be like that.' In other words, clean and in a certain order. My son says that I'm very closed minded.

> When I've finished washing, grooming myself, I get the cloth and clean everything up. The lady who comes to my house says 'Don't bother, I'll do it when I come.' But I can't stand the stains on the mirror from the toothpaste in those two days that she doesn't come.

Manolo's son Manolito shares his meticulous identity and approach to housework, already identified as a masculine approach in his own family: 'Dirt and disorder are both the same, its just that I'm really meticulous. I do it because I've got to or because it's necessary. I could sit and mend anything, but I do the cleaning because its a necessity.' For these men doing the housework was equally performative of their masculine identity as any other task that they might engage in would be. Because their performativity was expressive of what they represented as their natural or innate meticulous characters, it was through housework that they reaf-firmed their particular masculinity, using this sense of natural self to tran-scend natural metaphors of gender difference.

In describing these material and experiential aspects of their lives in their sensory homes, men informants also intentionally connected them to their self-identities. Their departures from traditional, housewifely and obsessive approaches are therefore also invested with specific narratives of masculinity, critiques of hegemonic masculinities, and statements about the sort of man each informant saw himself as naturally being. Above I have explored meticulous identities, below I suggest a series of other masculinities and homes that are emergent of the everyday performativity, intentionalities and self-identities informants described.

'Adventurous' Identities and Men's Sensory Knowledge

Beer concluded his introduction to *Househusbands* with a statement about how he reconciled his own masculinity with housework:

> Men can be good at housework, and the experience can often be a source of great personal and emotional satisfaction. At the same time, being involved in housework is not necessarily contradictory to manhood; a man does not have to become feminine to adapt. My own feeling is that doing housework makes me more of a man, because it is an adventure like others, with its tribulations and rewards. One of my hobbies is mountain climbing, and I have climbed all forty-six peaks over four thousand feet in the White Mountains of New Hampshire, as well as some peaks in the Rockies. A day of cooking, cleaning, childcare and household management is not unlike climbing a mountain. (Beer 1983: xxi)

Inviting other men to join in the masculine narrative of exploration and adventure that housework might become, he insisted: 'Housework may not be Everest, but it is an adventure that awaits any man who wants to forge ahead and meet the challenges of unexplored territory' (Beer 1983: xxi).

The idea of housework as an adventure also resonated amongst my men informants. To survive in this action-packed adventure world of housework a masculine hero might need powerful weapons and complex technologies. For instance, Malcolm told me that 'I know I need something that's sort of powerful and cheap. And I go to something that looks industrial and has a kind of DANGER DEATH! sign on it. I'll get something that looks like that.' In Spain and England men described housework as a journey into the unknown, that would sometimes be rationalized through science. In the Prologue I described how Malcolm was confronted with a dark, cold, smelly mess when he moved into his flat. Such experiences involved my informants dealing with and creating new sensations, smells, sights and textures. In doing so they engaged products and tools that enabled them to transform the sensory state of their homes. Adventure narratives represent men's housework as performative of a traditional heroic masculinity, and provide appropriate sensory metaphors through which men might speak about housework. Men who speak of housework as combined adventure and science narratives use masculine knowledge to interpret their home and housework processes, talking for instance of the relationship between metals, deposits and chemicals, as opposed to housewifely knowledge.

Men's adventure narratives were dominated by the inexplicable and unknown, focusing on mystery and danger. Some such stories were resolved through (pseudo) scientific explanations, but not all of these tales ended in science. Some remained suspended in mystery, particularly in the mystery of the power of non-human agency in and of the home as it is implicated in supernatural, natural and mystical processes. Some men constructed parts of the home, especially those related to housework, as supernatural or incomprehensible. Like the 'colourful growths' in Paul's kitchen and the 'funny smell' when Malcolm defrosted his freezer, these spaces and textures of home were not referred to in the terminology of rationality or science. Some informants implied that certain objects, technologies, textures and processes that occur in their homes had their own agency, personality and character (such as Malcolm's hoover and Gonzalo's sponge discussed in Chapter 2). Some of these were even mysterious, dangerous and not to be engaged with. For example Malcolm told me 'I stay away from the oven. I find them scary places – go there with a lighted match and you don't know what's going to happen.' Similarly Gonzalo mystified the processes by which dirt is produced and removed in his home by using natural and supernatural metaphors of fauna and the miraculous.

> I always spill my coffee, and that's normally dirty because I don't have time to clean it up, I mean I always spill my coffee, and I don't have time to clean it up, so when I get in its dried, and the stain gets bigger and creates its own fauna with a life of its own during the week . . . What I hate the most is the kitchen and the bathroom. I don't like them at all. Apart from the fact that they get very dirty, I don't know why, but they're always getting dirty. Then I love seeing it all clean, you know? When I get in and its clean, I say 'Wow, what a miracle', and you see it all shining, its perfect, but that only happens about once a month.

To resolve such mysteries some men depended on what Mario referred to as 'Mum power' – the women's expert housewifely knowledge I discussed in Chapter 5.

To sum up, the masculine adventure narrative is an interesting metaphor for housework as it involves both mysterious agencies and rational scientific resolutions. It offers an interpretation of the sensory world of housework that includes visual and olfactory effects and the embodied sensations that go with them. However, it need not conclude in science. Indeed some informants did not seek to identify themselves with rationality, but insisted that they did not possess the appropriate knowledge with which to resolve the incomprehensible aspects of housework. In doing so they were distinguishing themselves and their identities from feminine housewifeliness and what they saw as the housewife's ability to cope with any domestic mystery, and from a rational masculinity. Doubtless there were more complex reasons why each individual might distance himself from this masculine model. However, through these informants' unwillingness to engage with either of these potential solutions to domestic mysteries, they suggested the agency of smells, stains, growths, and ovens. In contrast men who, like Beer and his informants, engage with the full adventure narrative do their housework in ways that are performative of action-hero masculinities, thus making their housework expressive not only of their own sense of self, but, through metaphor, of a traditional masculinity.

Nonetheless most of my men informants respected the importance and utility of housewifely knowledge and solutions. Most men had a woman friend or relative who they would ask if they needed advice on running their homes. However, in doing so these men, like non-housewifely women, tended not to become involved in housewifely problem solving, but instead required a solution in the form of a method. As such they were not prepared to engage with understanding housewifely knowledge or processes, and in fact stated categorically that they just *did not* understand such matters. For example, Mario described how he was unable to understand the laundry instructions that his mother had given him. By thus naturalizing their inability to understand housework as a fixed and essential aspect of their characters, men distinguished their own housewifely practices from those of housewives. In doing so they did not necessarily propose that only women could achieve such feminine understandings (often noting that they knew women who had much worse attitudes to housework than they did). Nevertheless they *were* asserting that housewifely understandings were not comprehensible in terms of their own sensory and intellectual understandings of their environments.

Routines, Organization and Lazy Men

Although the masculine adventure narrative described by both English and Spanish men might imply spontaneity as opposed to routine, in fact their approaches to routine were strikingly similar to those of non-housewife women of their respective cultures. English women non-housewife informants saw routine as restricting, feeling housework should be motivated by their natural impulses, while Spanish women felt routine maintained a natural balance in their lives. Paul was a postgraduate student in England living in a shared student house and writing his dissertation. His approach to routine demonstrates some recurring differences between Spanish and English informants. For example at his present life-stage Paul prioritized his career plan above everyday routines:

> The real priority at the moment is to sort out what I'm doing in terms of career. You know, where I want to be, what I want to be doing because I can see it quite easily, on a daily basis, you put things off and put things off and it sort of doesn't get done and you don't end up being where you want to be at a certain time.

In Spain Juan, who lived alone, was also at a key moment, studying for his end of year Law degree exams. In contrast to Paul he set his pursuit of career success within the narrative of a daily routine:

> I get up, have shower, and start studying until my stomach starts to rumble – I start to get hungry. So I give myself a break, make lunch and then after I've eaten I might have a siesta depending on how stressed I am. But in the end before the siesta I clear away all the things I've cooked with or haven't cooked with and the things I've eaten with. Then if I've been sitting in the sofa I'll normally do that after the siesta. If I've had enough will power to just eat quickly in the kitchen so that I can't have a siesta, then I'll get everything done at the same time and then get back to studying later. Then I'll keep at it until about eight or something and then I like to go out in the garden or go running or do some sport. After some exercise I'll have a shower and then have dinner. I'll make whatever I've got for dinner and that's my routine more or less. And for dinner I'm usually in the living room, usually lounging on the sofa. I'll take the things through when I go to bed, usually I'll get the tray and leave it in the kitchen. I soak the things in water so they aren't really dirty and they won't be difficult to clean at breakfast time. Then I'll go to bed. That's a normal routine day.

The interviews showed how people's attitudes to routine also constitute part of their self-identities. Some English men informants who rejected routine spoke about this in terms of their independence from other people. Pete told me:

> There's no routine to it at all. It's just when I get to the point where I've been looking at dust rather than looking at something. I've put fresh flowers in there, this weekend. I like flowers and I get flowers and put them in there but

the dead flowers from the last bunch are still on the floor. I walk past that every day of my life and don't do it. Still there comes a point where everything is so untidy, dusty, I think I've had enough, I'VE had enough of living here, it's not because somebody else is coming.

Some men were particularly concerned with the presentation of their home to others, and with how people might judge their homes. In England where men had more visitors at home, they often inserted housework into a social narrative. Housework could form part of a sensory 'going out' narrative that involved a man preparing himself for a night out and preparing his home in case he did not return alone. Others incorporated housework into a more everyday social pattern. For example, Ben lived alone in London in a studio flat, aged thirty-two at the time. He saw himself as untidy and living in an 'organized mess'. He usually had friends round for drinks about twice a week and friends from outside London to stay every month. Ben's housework formed part of this social narrative of having visitors. Rather than following a housework routine, he cleaned when expecting visitors; therefore his continual flow of friends organized his domestic life for him:

> I'm quite lazy when it comes to cleaning so I tend to clean before I have a visitor as opposed to particular times of the week or anything. So it's quite a good trick, if I have a visitor coming and I know within a day or two before that and whizz around with the hoover and the duster and that's OK.

Like English women, men consistently suggested they were lazy at home, seeking motivation, like Ben, from social narratives or, like Paul, from natural impulses. This self-representation as lazy was thus embedded in their actual timing of housework and similarly expressive of their departures from the obsessive approaches I discussed above. Spanish men did not tend to speak of their attitudes to their homes in terms of laziness. For instance Javier was thirty-three, a teacher who lived alone in his own two-bedroom flat. His response was quite typical of other Spanish men of different ages who rented or owned their homes. He felt it was important to keep his home organized and worked to a routine. Javier cleaned the bathroom daily: 'normally when I have a shower, when I shave, I clean the sink, I'm careful'. He washed up his plates after eating every day and did some tidying up at lunchtimes. On Saturdays he cleaned the flat thoroughly. He would occasionally postpone the housework in favour of his social life, but Javier saw housework as having a particular place in his life and would not normally allow other narratives to change this. Unlike some English informants, neither would he put off his work by cleaning:

Sarah: If you've got a lot of grading to do, and you don't feel like it, would you start cleaning?

Javier: No, I'd do my grading, I mean, I wouldn't clean just to clean for its own sake. I try to clean so that things are clean, not for fun. But, perhaps in a couple of hours I've done the whole house.

Even Gonzalo, who said he 'hated' housework, did not subordinate the housework to his emotional narrative. Rather, he explained the link between his own feelings and housework as fortunate if they coincided:

Gonzalo: Often, I get up very early on Saturday mornings, and when I'm in a temper its perfect, because if I'm in a bad mood, I clean much faster and I put a lot more energy into it.

Sarah: Does cleaning get rid of your bad mood?

Gonzalo: Well, no.

Sarah: No?

Gonzalo: No, but I do get some of it off my chest. I tire myself out, because you tire yourself out, and when you're tired out, then . . . the thing is, I don't normally get angry.

Both English and Spanish men felt they organized their housework according to their own personalities and priorities. Whilst most English men identified their approaches to housework as lazy, Spanish men took up housework processes and routines with more vigour and rigour. Emphasizing the importance of cleanliness for a balanced life, they also related their approaches to housework to their natural selves. As for the women discussed in Chapter 6, these approaches represent culturally different notions of having a balanced life.

Masculine Homes? Masculine Identities and the Multiple Agencies of Home

Men often linked their home creativity to narratives of identity and a sense of a natural self that housework and home decoration accommodated (rather than *vice versa*). In homemaking men engage in an activity that has been gendered feminine, yet do so in ways they feel are expressive of their own personalities. Some mentioned their own attention to detail, laziness, or aesthetic tastes. They reflexively embedded their discussions of their present home decoration in biographical narratives of self, family and home. Thus they represented not only the changing home but changing relationships, moralities and 'philosophies on life' they felt were interwoven with their homes. They created narratives about themselves and their homes that formed consistent accounts of self-identity. In doing so they generated meanings that were invested in objects, structures, music, radio, smell, sights and touch. In the Prologue I outlined how Malcolm interwove his discussion of his home decoration with his philosophy of life. His home was intentionally expressive of his argument that one might create a home on a next-to-nothing budget, and constituted an anti-materialist statement. However, he was constrained by the condition of the flat and the resources available, and inspired by the help of friends. Rather than simply expressive of the individual men's creativity, their homes are also shaped by economic contexts, material structures and other social agencies.

For example, despite wanting to settle down, Ben had 'always' travelled, had participated in school exchange programmes and studied languages as a student. He spoke several languages, had lived and travelled extensively in Africa, and was shortly leaving for a European trip. The years he spent in Africa impacted on how he lived in his home and were represented in his decoration, music and the smells and tastes of his cooking. Travel also figured in how Ben socialized in his home, with frequent visits from friends from abroad or travelling to the airport. Ben's kitchen was tiny and inconvenient, nevertheless, like many English kitchens, was personalized, decorated with photographs of friends from abroad. As he explained how he organized his kitchen, Ben simultaneously described his social life at home and the objects from his travels. His kitchen was not simply expressive of his social life and travel experiences, but constituted by them in negotiation with its structure and facilities. As we explored the contents of his kitchen cupboards, I asked about his coffee display situated on the grill, which, as he never used it, doubled up as a shelf:

> Yes, I have a variety of coffees that have come in to me from Africa. This one was bought in Ethiopia. I have a friend who's a specialist consultant with Christian Aid and he flies off through Addis Ababa occasionally and brings me coffee back. And then this one I brought back from Kenya, a couple of months ago. And then that one came from Spain fairly recently.

The social and structural elements of his home life had also impacted on the present appearance of his kitchen:

> I've had a few friends round this morning and I've not got round to washing cups yet. Nothing too grim. Kettle, I've actually nowhere to put the kettle so it just sits on the draining board. I guess it should be sitting on top of something else actually. I think there's a bit dangerous with water and stuff but, erm, you know. And then this [a wooden pestle and mortar] comes from

Africa . . . I put garlic in there and pound my garlic and other things occasionally.

Ben used indigenous handmade West African cooking utensils alongside the English kettle and utensils that also inhabited his cramped draining board. These African utensils were not simply ornamental souvenirs, but were incorporated alongside the technologies of a modern western kitchen. Thus appropriated they had roles and meanings constituted by how they were situated and used in relation to other objects. Women's displays of artefacts from their travels might stand for a departure from the gendering of public and domestic space as respectively masculine and feminine. In Ben's case, this departure is also evident as he integrates his travel objects into his everyday domestic life. His treatment of such artefacts also breaks traditional models. They are not the publicly displayed prizes of a masculine collector's narrative. They become domestic *subjects* that are *involved in* food preparation, and thus in the production of everyday life and home, rather that being a collection or *objects* to be looked at. As such they are incorporated as tactile, rather than simply visual elements of his experience of home.

The men discussed above saw their homes as expressive of their interests, tastes and beliefs. Pete took this further to emphasize how his home expressed something essential about his natural self. Aged fifty, Pete lived with his two student children. His home meant a lot to him, as a permanent stable base, where he felt secure and happy. He decorated his living room with pictures and ornaments that 'mean something' to him, mainly gifts from his children and relatives that map out his social world. Pete's approach to home decoration was performative of the self-identity he represented as 'perhaps secretly lazy' and 'naturally' easily bored. He showed me his half-painted dining room, explaining that:

> I sit here and make plans about, you know, making the place really nice . . . but I can't motivate myself to spend a weekend making it nice . . . I plan to decorate rooms and I just never, I mean you'll see this room – I've obviously painted half the ceiling, half the wall! I've got an incredibly low boredom threshold. I'll set my stall out to paint that room and by lunchtime on Saturday I'll be so pissed off with it that I'll go and do something else. And if somebody rings up and says do you fancy a pint? No contest! I'm gone.

Pete saw this approach as natural to him, 'not something deliberate', and impossible to change. Without his intervention, wallpaper 'peels off' and mould 'accumulates' between the bathroom tiles. These agencies produced textures of home that he said he was naturally powerless to control. Thus he understood his home an expression of his true self. Comparing himself with meticulous or housewifely friends, he saw their motivation and sensory knowledge as incomprehensible and inaccessible to him: 'when I go to my friends' houses and other people's houses are really nice, I'm really envious. I think "this is really nice". But I just can't begin to understand how they keep it like that.'

My Spanish men informants similarly felt their homes were expressive of their personal tastes, characters and diverse masculine identities. In his rented flat Gonzalo had made some of his own furniture and most of his art and image compositions were either his own work or by artist friends. He felt he had created a home that, although not ideal, was a space he was happy in. In doing so he had challenged what he regarded as the more conventional or traditional values of his family: 'my family hate this flat. They say that its really small, that its a bird coop . . . that its shabby, that its this and that . . . But I feel good here.' Whilst recognizing that he enjoyed the experience of relaxing on the sofa and watching the large TV when he visited his sister or parents, Gonzalo insisted that he gave more value to his outdoor *terraza*. This was a space where he could relax, enjoy his own space, breathe the night air and be creative artistically and musically. In doing so he was also making it clear that he did not want to have the traditional home that his relatives lived in and that his priorities and values were different. The outdoor atmosphere and his careful choices of music, furniture and images combined to create his sensory home, compensating for aspects of that flat he felt were not totally ideal. Although some Spanish men informants prided themselves in being dexterous with small DIY jobs, most, like Gonzalo, focused their creativity on other aspects of home-making. They hired paid experts to do carpentry and other jobs in their homes. When I interviewed Javier, who was also thirty-two, he had lived in his own flat for a year. Little by little he was changing the flat; he had added shelving and innovated to adapt furniture to his own purposes, although, like Gonzalo, not in a DIY sense, insisting that he was not interested in or good at DIY. Rather, Javier enjoyed cooking and was happy with the feel and look of his beautiful new kitchen with a marble floor and a special hob. Like the English men I discussed above, Spanish men also tended to link their home creativity to their natural selves. Manolo, who saw himself as meticulous. had been careful to alter his recently purchased flat, making some structural changes so that it would be *exactly* as he wanted it, and commissioning new furniture and a mobile television stand to suit his purposes.

Men's home creativity and the negotiations they entered into with social, material and sensory agencies of home were usually personalized and often related to identity issues. As the examples above demonstrate, men's approaches often ran counter to traditional versions of feminine domesticity. However, as Miller (2001b) has suggested men were also 'haunted' by ex-tenants, architectural design, the biography of the home, and external agencies such as landlords and co-tenants. Men living in rented accommodation frequently had to contend with complex cocktails of such agencies. For example, Paul said that although he was not obsessive about housework, house sharing had required him to lower his standards. He and his housemates kept housework, decoration and maintenance to a minimum, not because they were dirty or unimaginative, but because these activities were enmeshed in a complex relationship with the landlord, condition of the house and ex-tenants. Birdwell-Pheasant and Lawrence-Zúñiga argue that 'much of what family and household members experience as the physical structure of the house is in fact the collective outcome of the agency of others, especially in the past' (1999: 9). Paul's relationship to the bathroom, which was mediated by his relationship to his housemates and landlord, can be understood in these terms. Paul neither felt responsible for the state of the bathroom nor saw it as reflection of himself, but as expressive of the landlord's 'not caring, to be honest with you, not meeting us halfway at all'. He told me the landlord had promised to fit a new bathroom for several years: 'If he [the landlord] sorted out a new bathroom then we'd probably be more inclined to clean it up. Because it's a mess to start off with, yes you don't really take much pride in it, to be honest . . . I mean this is pretty much the, never bother cleaning it cos the landlord hasn't changed it.'

Seeing himself as a clean person, having grown up in his mother's clean home, Paul was clearly physically and emotionally uncomfortable with a bathroom that he felt was essentially unclean: 'If there was ever a room I was kind of embarrassed about it would be the bathroom because it is filthy. It's always a mess even if it's really, even if it's actually clean – it's not dirty – then it's still a mess, just from the structure of it.' We discussed the sensory and embodied experience of using his bathroom and he described how he negotiated his use of it accordingly:

Paul: I usually have a shower, I wouldn't use it for a bath.
Sarah: Why's that then?
Paul: Well it's just dirty, it's just dirty and it needs a clean. It just looks old and nasty, so I wouldn't use it for anything. But the one I use basically, is in here, I have a shower, clean my teeth, stuff like that so it doesn't bother me too much.
Sarah: And what about the tiles and that?
Paul: I mean I've sort of resigned myself to it.
Sarah: And are there parts of it that, you know, you just wouldn't touch?

> How do you feel about it being in this state, because obviously
> you've got to use it?
>
> *Paul:* Yes, exactly. Plus it's the place where, you know, you clean your-
> self and that sort of thing. I wouldn't, it doesn't feel comfortable,
> being in here, obviously.
>
> *Sarah:* You wouldn't like have a relaxing bath?
>
> *Paul:* Oh God, no, no. Just have a shower.

Paul felt it was inappropriate for him or his housemates to improve the
bathroom and because of this was also reluctant to clean it. His approach
to housework and decoration in his own room was a strong contrast. Here
he kept his academic books and work and his computer. In negotiation
with the landlord he had painted the walls. White, not his preferred colour,
had been a compromise so he had subsequently covered the walls with
pictures and posters, but Paul's own agency intersected with other material
and social agencies to produce an outcome he felt represented his identity
more strongly. In other rooms this balance shifted as the agency of 'the
house', as a biographical, material and social entity, came into play.
Halloween decorations and posters in the living and dining areas and
tinned foods in a cupboard were 'leftovers' from previous parties and
tenants: 'remnants of people who have lived here previously'. Because
these were the responsibility of 'no one' they were perceived as pertaining
to 'the house', and part of the environment, rather than the outcome of the
agency of the current housemates. In contrast to informants who 'blitzed'
and bleached their new homes on moving in, in communal rooms the
housemates deferred to 'the house', including the landlord, 'remnants'
from ex-housemates, and some of their own additions.

In Simon's case his personal priorities inspired him to keep his flat
clean and tidy (see above). Nevertheless his relationship to the letting
agency also mediated what he was 'prepared to do':

> *Simon:* I haven't got a headboard on my bed. I've asked them for that,
> countless times, when I first came in. It never came and I've just
> given up now. I've never had one.
>
> *Sarah:* I mean don't those sort of things affect your attitude towards the
> flat?
>
> *Simon:* Er, I suppose, yes, I'll keep it clean but I won't go over the top . . .
> I wouldn't go as far as to repaint the window frames or anything
> else. And I wouldn't really improve it in any way. I put a shower, a
> shower fitting into the bathroom but I think when I move out I'll
> probably take it with me. I won't leave it here. So, yes it's that
> whole thing about not owning a place. It's not my place so you
> know I can't really be bothered and I haven't got the time.

In his living room Simon represented his interests through posters and pictures of his musical, film and sporting tastes and the music he played. Here he appropriated the props of housewifely activity to support objects that represented his own interests and projects. Keyboards stood on his ironing board and a computer stood on the dining room table. Simultaneously he suggested both disrespect for the pinewood table that he disliked, and a disregard for the traditional uses of this and other objects by engaging them thus.

In Chapter 6 I described how my women informants engaged creatively with the various agencies of their homes in a series of negotiations from which both home and gender might be seen as emergent. Men were similarly involved in home decoration, and sensory interpretation and creativity of their homes. Those men informants who cleaned and decorated their homes less did not do so simply because they felt that such work was 'women's work' but for reasons that they saw as particular to themselves as individuals or because of their relationships to other agencies of home. English and Spanish men informants created home in a variety of ways contingent on the other material, sensory and social agencies – structures, objects, smells, textures, landlords, co-tenants, partners and so on – they contended with.

Men and the Sensory Agencies of Home

In Chapter 6 I emphasized how the women I interviewed dealt with the dilemma of performing activities associated with traditional femininity in ways that resisted the discourses and moralities of traditional gender. When men engage in housework and home creativity they are faced with a different dilemma: how do they perform traditionally feminine tasks in ways that are expressive of their masculinity? The examples I have discussed in this chapter have shown how English and Spanish men have done so by departing from obsessive approaches, using the metaphors of adventure narratives and the sensory embodied experience that these entail to frame their housework experiences. They referred their approaches to personal characteristics that are essential to them as individuals and in doing so described how their home creativity challenged traditional and gendered uses of space and artefacts.

A comparison of my English and Spanish men informants shows that, as for women, their approaches to routine differed according to culturally specific understandings. However, there were many commonalities in how Spanish and English men represented the sensory experience of adventure housework. The themes of the living textures of home (mould and growths), the tactile floor (see Chapter 4) and the animation of technologies

(Chapter 2) resonated through the interviews. Men attributed imaginary agency to these aspects of the sensory home whereas women did not. In other situations they located agency in the essential natures of their (culturally specific) personalities – things they 'couldn't help' – such as being meticulous or lazy. As such, men situated their own agency in the home rather differently to non-housewifely women who were much more indignant about their having taken control in a way that allowed them to 'get on with my life' and might mean not doing the housework. This in part explains why men often attached their experiences to an adventure narrative – a classic local tale that has been represented in global Indiana Jones type narratives only to be reappropriated locally. Their use of such a narrative means their sensory and intellectual experiences and under-standings of the home are constructed and represented quite differently from women's.

8

Conclusion: Sensory Knowledge and Creative Practices

Writing this book has involved the transformation of applied research into an academic text. Some 'purists' might propose that two such projects are incompatible. In anticipation of such comments I would argue that this ethnographic study, the design, research practice and analysis of which was informed by anthropological principles and theory, qualifies as well as any other to form the basis for an academic argument. Simultaneously, however, such work is subject to different constraints from those encountered in 'pure' (or purely) academic work, and below I discuss some of the issues this raises. First I outline the argument developed in the preceding chapters. Then I draw together two themes that resonate throughout the book to discuss the roles of knowledge and routine in changing gendered practices and identities. Finally I outline the wider implications of this work for anthropology.

Themes and Issues

In the previous chapters I have interlinked a series of themes and questions. First I proposed that a theory of gender performativity and individual creativity can offer insights in how a wider context of changing gender is constituted through everyday practices in the home. Second I argued that the home should be treated as a pluri-sensory context. As such we should attend to how everyday experiences and practices in the home depend on sensory knowledge, and are represented in terms of sensory metaphor. Finally I reported on how traditional housewifely identities and new masculinities and femininities are being maintained and are emerging in the context of the home in England and Spain. Here I summarize my argument and the interlinkages between the questions dealt with in the book.

I initially conceived this book as a project about changing Spanish and English masculinities and femininities and how these were constituted in the home. This in itself is not such an original project as the relationship between identity and home (although often without the gender focus) is well established in existing work. However, my research (see Chapter 2) convinced me that the key to understanding the relationship between identity and home lies not only in processes of appropriation (Miller 1988), 'estate agency' (Miller 2001b) and 'accommodation' (Miller 2002), but in the embodied experience of home and the sensory knowledge and metaphors used to inform action in, and representations of, the home. To understand more fully how people experience and objectify their gender identities in the home I needed to focus on how they constructed not just their own sensory practices and self-identities but also the alterity of those whose embodied knowledge and moralities differed from theirs. A theory of gender performativity outlined in Chapter 3 provided me with a way of understanding how contesting gendered identities might be constituted through domestic practices. Then I explored how sensory embodied knowledge and practice were part of this performativity in Chapter 4. Putting these ideas into practice in Chapters 5–7 I could understand, first, how non-housewife informants constructed the housewife and situated themselves in relation to her and, second, the types of sensory knowledge they were prepared to assimilate and to use to inform their own embodied housework and home creativity practices. It is through these practices and their departures from convention that changing masculinities and femininities emerge.

Using this approach I have shown how housewives use sensory experience and knowledge to describe and inform their housework and home creativity. These sensory practices continually maintain and/or transform the textures, smells, sounds and sights of their homes within the constraints set by their sensory and material environments. Attached to particular 'traditional' moralities, the practices not only serve to create and maintain the home, but are performative of culturally specific housewifely identities – identities that are constituted and reconstituted through the everyday repetition of their sensory embodied practices of home. These practices are culturally informed with knowledge about the sensory qualities of elements of the home, as I have shown in the example of dust in Chapter 4. However, significantly, as I outlined in Chapter 5, both in England and Spain housewives spoke of a housework routine as significantly structuring their everyday lives. Women informants who rejected a housewife identity constructed housewives simultaneously as 'obsessive' and as experts who had access to privileged sensory knowledge and strategies. For instance a housewife would see dirt that they could not. She would also be able to solve the problem of how to remove a stain or sticky surface that they could not. Indeed they told me that they would clean their homes to sensory cues that did not form part of a housewife's sensory repertoire. Whereas for a housewife a 'smelly' sink or fridge would be a problem out of hand, for them it was part of a process of renewal and transformation. In Chapter 6 I described how above all English women rejected the idea of following a housewifely domestic routine, insisting that their own spur for doing housework was a more embodied need that connected physical work with everyday emotional narratives. When 'in the mood' they found cleaning therapeutic. As such they made housework serve them. At the same time, they recognized that at times they needed the expert knowledge of the housewife. However, rather that engaging with the full embodied and sensory knowledge that informed the practices of the housewife they preferred to take a pragmatic approach. As such they developed practices based on following a housewife's instructions while disengaged from the housewifely knowledge that made these comprehensible. Spanish women took a similar approach, differing mainly in their attitudes to routine. They saw a structured routine as positive, bringing a natural balance between different areas of one's life. These cultural differences in understanding routine also ran through my analysis of men's interviews and I return to the question of routine below. However, both Spanish and English men not only disengaged with housewifely knowledge, emphasising alternative sensory ways of knowing when to clean, but also tended to invent their own sensory knowledge narratives though which to speak about their experiences and practices of housework and home creativity. These linked to sensory adventure narratives that lent agency to textures, growths, objects and chemicals in the home. They also rooted their approaches by essentializing aspects of their individual identities, such as being 'independent' or 'meticulous'. As I argued in Chapter 7, my men informants in Spain and England framed their departures from housewifery differently to my women non-housewife informants. Women were involved in representing how they used their female bodies to perform domestic tasks while rejecting a traditional feminine role. This meant they needed to create an alternative embodied femininity. In contrast men could easily incorporate masculine narratives of embodied adventures into their representations and practices because they were involved in creating a masculinity that did housework in ways that were both personal and/or masculine, but that did not feminize the male body that was performing traditionally feminine tasks.

Sensory Knowledge, Informed Practice and Contesting the Norm

Few anthropologists have been concerned with the relationship between the senses and practice.[1] However, as I have shown here, sensory

experience and understanding are key elements that inform the performance of everyday actions. Two related themes emerge from the summary
above. First, how different people engage with sensory knowledge to
inform their domestic practices, and, second, how gender is constituted
through sensory embodied practice. This relationship between knowledge, identity and practice is key to understanding how indviduals
perform their gendered selves and construct gendered others.
Housewives, to greater or lesser degrees, were seen by others and saw
themselves as repositories and users of specialist knowledge. They have
particular ways of understanding the home that can be learnt but that likewise others might reject learning about. More generally ways of learning
and understanding sensory practices are not purely intellectual but
involve the acquisition of sensory knowledge and skills. For example in
my previous fieldwork in Spain (1992–4) I learnt that gaining an understanding of the bullfight required not only a particular way of visually
'seeing' the performance but an ability to empathize with the sensory
embodied experience of the bullfighter (see Pink 1997a). This would
mean for example sensing the sound of music, imagining the smell and
force of the proximity of the bull, and projecting oneself in the bullfighter's body as he performed the cape passes. All this would require a
certain amount of training in performing the passes oneself and study of
actual performances. The same might be said for an understanding of
housewifely knowledge and practice. This understanding involves learning not simply a way of seeing, but a way of experiencing and acting with
the whole sensory body. Linked to this is a way of understanding that
classifies sensory experience and practice according to particular sensory
modalities. By using the 'right' sensory modality to assess the cleanliness
of the home a housewife is not simply engaging in a skilled sensory practice but also referring to a moral discourse.

   Unlike public performances such as the bullfight, housewifely practices
are usually undertaken by indviduals working alone in their homes. Each
housewife has her own unique way of doing, and feeling about, her housework. Nevertheless, as Oakley's (1974) study showed, different housewives feelings about housework were quite similar (see Chapter 5). The
knowledge housewives employ is shared, to the degree that the housewives
I interviewed discussed and exchanged knowledge with other like-minded
women in their family and friendship networks. They also endeavoured to
teach (although not always successfully) their children some of their
knowledge. In Chapters 4–7 I discussed how non-housewives treat housewifely skills, sensory knowledge and understandings. I emphasized that
those people who 'never' spoke about their housework to anyone rejected
the housewifely expertise they had witnessed housewives (often their

mothers, but also other women) employ. Significantly they were unwilling to learn and engage with the knowledge that would enable them to perform housewifely practice. Instead they asked housewives for solutions (rather than knowledge and understanding) to isolated housework problems, such as how to clean particular new domestic object or remove a specific stain. Mario, in his late twenties, who saw himself as incapable of understanding the principles of (normative) housewifely practice, is good example. Mario overturned the conventions of my housewifely informants in the way he assessed his laundry. He smelt, touched and visually examined it using embodied practices very unlike those of my housewife informants, and applied sensory metaphors that draw from a very different vocabulary to theirs. Mario is not unusual either in performing an eclectic set of practices or being unconnected to others who might share his practices. The only person he reported discussing laundry with was a woman colleague who had advised him on the quantity of powder to use. His use of powder was informed by housewifely advice, but did not involve him engaging the knowledge it was based on. In this case he, quite typically for my non-housewife informants, used sensory knowledge and metaphor that was not based on housewifely expertise to assess his laundry, and asked a housewife for a pragmatic solution to his dilemma concerning how much powder to use. It is not the case that these informants *never* shared any knowledge about housework with others. As I have shown people who reject a housewifely identity also have many practices and approaches in common. However, it is clear that they do not participate in personal or family networks or communities focused on, or frequently interact and share knowledge about, housework. Instead I would argue that their practices are constituted through their culturally informed and creative ways of departing from their own models of housewifery.

To sum up, individuals engage with and/or reject particular categories of sensory knowledge that they associate with housewifely or 'independent'/'balanced' practice. They use this sensory knowledge to inform their everyday actions at home. Moreover the sensory cues they use to inspire them to do housework are attached to particular sets of values, and challenge others. Through their creative sensory practices they might contest convention and produce the new gendered identities that are represented in the changing gender profiles of Spain and England. By focusing on the different sensory modalities through which people represent their domestic experiences, knowledge and practices we can open up paths to understanding how they employ types of knowledge that are not apparent in research that attends only to the visual/material home.

Routine, Anti-routine and Changing Practices

The sensory knowledge and practices discussed above, however, need to be set within a wider framework of activity that shapes and organizes them temporally. Thus to situate changing gender and practice requires an engagement with both my informants' perspectives on routine and existing theories of routine. In Chapter 3 I noted how my non-housewife informants represented their own deviations from routines or their perceived lack of routine as evidence of their independence. In Chapters 5–7 this was developed further. We saw how housewife routines were constructed and rejected by women and men informants alike in culturally specific ways in England and Spain. My informants interpreted routine as meaning a structured predetermined set of activities that would be repeated on a weekly or daily basis. Working with this concept, English non-housewife informants conceived their own narratives as anti-routine. Spanish non-housewife informants, in contrast, valued routine but contested its frequency. Theoretically routine has been addressed predominantly in the sociological literature. Notably, Giddens has argued that it is through reflexively monitored everyday routines that individuals maintain control in everyday life. Indeed for him 'the subject cannot be grasped save through the reflexive constitution of daily activities in social practices'. This is crucial for Giddens' theory of structuration because he claims routine both maintains 'the continuity of the personality of the agent' and the 'institution of society' (1984: 60). Thus, he claims, routines serve to maintain order, and are unchanging even in times of crisis, like revolution (Giddens 1984: 87). Giddens' formulation, as Shove's analysis (2003: 161–2) of how the challenge of new technologies can lead to collective adoptions of new routines illustrates, is too static. Moreover, as Garvey notes, Giddens' model problematically negates the individual spontaneity (2001: 54) which might break routine. Garvey considers her informants' sporadic rearrangements of furniture in their homes. These, performed on a repetitive basis, might be seen as a form of routine. However, such practices cannot be seen as necessarily maintaining existing forms, but might also instigate change. My informants defined routine as regular daily or weekly repetition of specific practices. In contrast housework practices that were performed repetitively, but not at predetermined times, were classified as anti-routine. A second means of rejecting routine was to fill a conventional routine with practices that were themselves unconventional. Finally a conventional routine might be resisted by inserting longer gaps between the actions it entails. Anthropologically these latter, anti-routine, systems of organization of practices might be defined as a form of routine in themselves: they *are* embedded in structured personal narratives. However, following my informants' distinction between routine and anti-routine, it is precisely the anti-routine that references and challenges conventional routine. The anti-routine offers a new basis ('personal' – essentializing one's character – and 'natural' ways of doing things) for everyday organization narratives. It thus proposes an alternative new routine. In these new routines particular sexed bodies and gendered identities selectively employ sensory knowledge and the values linked to it to undertake tasks that are conventionally performed by the housewife. By re-setting these tasks within the narratives created by the anti-routine in a way that was informed by sensory knowledge and personal emotional narrative and balance, my informants were able to engage in domestic practices that at the same time constituted performances of masculinities and femininities that resisted convention.

Processes of change thus encompass the co-existence of different (and sometimes contesting) practices informed by sensory knowledge, involving sensory action and set within diverse routines. They involve the whole, interconnected, sensory body and are made sense of through various different and contesting systems of sensory classification. Practices are moreover gendered and embodied and the way they are carried out concerns the performance of particular gendered identities with particular sexed bodies. Whether one experiences doing a house-wifely feminine task though a male or female body can be crucial to how one interprets that task performatively in practice, which sensory knowledge one uses to inform the action and to how one represents it to others. Examining how individuals situate themselves (both verbally and through practice) in relation to what they perceive as established housewifely or normative sensory knowledge and practice reveals how changing gender and practices are unevenly textured and are importantly to do with individual creativity and agency. This, however, does not mean we can say nothing about change other than that there is diversity. Indeed what is becoming important is the notion of a 'natural balance' (whether driven by routine or personal impulses and character) and independence. As such, new forms of domestic routine are emerging. It is this diversity and departure from housewifely sensory knowledge and practices based on balance and independence that are 'hidden' by the Spanish and British statistics on changing gender and by broader analyses of shifts in convention and practice.

Wider Implications

In the previous sections I have summed up the findings of my research and, by comparing them with those of similar work, outlined what we might learn about the dynamics of changing gender and sensory knowledge. My analysis has been based on an applied study and here I comment on some issues concerning the relationship between applied and academic anthropology. This study also has wider implications for the four main areas of anthropology the research and analysis drew from: the anthropology of the senses, the home and gender, and visual anthropology.

Producing an anthropological monograph based on an applied project is unusual and, I suspect, a practice that some academics will find problematic. However, in assessing the value of such an exercise its is more useful to reflect on opportunities, as well as constraints, that are not part of usual academic research. We are working in a context where the application of anthropology outside academia is increasingly in demand in public, private and non-governmental organizations. In this situation a growing number of anthropological studies that are funded by non-academic sponsors, yet which are informed by anthropological method and theory, are being produced. More often than not such work does not reach an academic sphere. Nevertheless, the discipline might benefit from a greater engagement with this work both empirically and methodologically.

Collaboration with researchers working outside academia can provide a rich combination of expertise and interest. One can expect public, private and non-governmental organizations that invest considerably in research to have impressive resources of expertise and materials in the areas that concern them. Their research may follow pathways of contemporary relevance that academics (who may have limited time and resources for research themselves) have not yet taken up – both empirically and methodologically. By commissioning research, organizations open up opportunities for an exchange of ideas and expertise between their own researchers and academics, creating new areas for academic study. My collaborations inspired my eventual focus on the sensory home and enabled me to develop new visual methodologies. Working to an agenda to produce results that will serve the client's needs might be seen as a constraint in that research questions and projects need to be framed so they can, within budget, produce what is required. However, such framing is not necessarily a bad thing as there are usually good empirical reasons that inform organizations' research priorities – which could well guide academics to fruitful new areas of investigation. Reports on the findings of such work are of course not enough to constitute an academic contribution. Nor indeed are they enough for a client as any applied project must be presented to its potential user in a form that will make it accessible and relevant. Likewise the essential academic task entails identifying where applied work can usefully contribute to anthropological thought – below I detail the main issues that my research has raised for academic anthropology. Nonetheless the scope of applied projects, and hence the academic impact they can have, is constrained to some degree. For example, applied work is often short-term and lacks the additional layers of research and analysis that situate its core findings. Anthropologists' previous fieldwork experience and knowledge of the cultures and themes they are working with compensate for this to some extent. Nevertheless long-term research allows one to deepen a project with comprehensive reviews and further participant observation. Applied projects cannot usually incorporate such longer time scales or their budget implications. The research discussed in this book is situated academically via its relationship to existing research and its methodological and theoretical implications. As such, as it stands it is intended to propose and invite a focus on the home as a sensory domain. It might also be extended to construct a more comprehensive framework for the anthropological study of the sensory home, which could include investigating historical dimensions, examining how everyday practices are interwoven with media culture, and looking to possibilities for interdisciplinary collaborative areas. In the following paragraphs of this section, I outline the themes and issues that this research has identified and the directions they invite future research to take.

A shift in the way anthropologists treat other people's sensory worlds is already starting to take place. Although in general anthropologists (perhaps especially visual anthropologists) have attended insufficiently to the senses other than the visual, the key works of Classen, Howes and Synnott (1994), Stoller (1989, 1997), Seremetakis (1994) and Ingold (2000), all discussed above, are having an impact. For example, in recent years Bubandt's (1998) study of olfaction in Indonesia, Desjarlais' study of sensory narratives in Tibet (2003), and Geurts' (e.g. 2002) work on the Anlo-Ewe understanding of sensory experience in Ghana have brought the senses to the forefront. In Britain Tacchi's work on domestic soundscapes (e.g. 1998) and Rice's acoustemology of the Edinburgh Royal Infirmary (2003) demonstrate the importance of seeking out how non-visual sensory experience, understanding and knowledge are relevant in particular contexts. My study of changing gender in the sensory home confirms the points made by these authors: in my view anthropologists need to acknowledge the sensory context in which we work, in both the modern west and other cultures, and to always be conscious of the idea that even in modern western contexts the visual/visible and material/tangible might not always be the only or most relevant source of knowledge. In this book I have taken this question further to argue that to understand modern western experience we need to focus not only on one sensory modality and its importance in a particular cultural or institutional context. Rather we might also learn much about how identities that both contest or reaffirm convention are constituted from variations in individual, cultural and gendered uses of sensory metaphor and action within the same or similar contexts.

The sub-discipline of anthropology of the home provides a good example of a field that this sensory approach might be applied to. Existing work on the home focuses on materiality and visuality (e.g. Miller 2002, Clarke 2002), usually without engaging with the wider sensory contexts. Therefore such work provides important insights into how people objectify their identities in their homes, but is limited in what it can tell us because it only focuses on one aspect of sensory understanding and knowledge. Some anthropologists of home have made important moves towards incorporating other sensory modalities. For example Hecht (2001) and Tacchi (1998) have looked at the sensory evocation of biographical memories of home and domestic soundscapes respectively. However, none of this work engages with the idea that people's experiences, understandings and knowledge of the home are embodied and multi or pluri-sensory. As I have demonstrated in the previous chapters, in fact much of the experience, knowledge and action that people engage with in their homes is conceived in terms of the non-visual senses. It is essential to recognize the wider sensory context of the home. Indeed, manufacturers of household goods have long needed to consider sensory experience and perception both to develop and market their products. It is time anthropologists of the home followed their example.

The work has similar implications for anthropological studies of gender and gendered knowledge. It is commonly acknowledged that gender is experienced corporally (usually) through male or female sexed bodies. There are some corporeal experiences that are accessible only to either male or female bodies. Aspects specific to sexual reproduction such as ejaculation and childbirth are perhaps the most obvious examples. However, it might also be argued that housework is a different corporeal experience for persons with male and female bodies and that therefore the sensory embodied experience of housework entails a different range of possibilities for male and female bodies. Femininity and masculinity are not necessarily experienced through female and male bodies respectively. Attention is due to the intersection between the corporal experience of the biologically sexed body and the way gender identities are constituted in relation to that embodied experience. Much knowledge is produced and used through embodied experience that involves sensory engagements with the environment. Such knowledge is experienced by sexed bodies and is gendered itself as it is associated with different identity types. To understand how the multiple femininities and masculinities that make up the contemporary gender pattern are lived, I suggest it is instructive to account for how sensory experiences, knowledge, metaphors, meanings and actions are bound up with this. Desjarlais (2003) demonstrates how his Tibetan male and female informants' gendered biographies of life in the same culture were told though quite different sensory metaphors. Comparisons of the ways in which different people living within the same culture tell their own identity stories though particular sensory metaphors and describe the sensory worlds and knowledge systems they see themselves as living in can provide important insights. They can not only illuminate how men and women might experience similar contexts in different ways, but also focus on how such experiences differ within each gender, as identities are crosscut by age, economic and social class, ethnicity and so forth. For example one can begin to imagine how the sensory experience of the same home would be different for the professional working mother who owns it and the immigrant women she pays to clean it. Such an approach holds potential for examining how gender inequalities (between and amongst women and men) are experienced in everyday life, not only through visual and narrative representations, but also as embodied realities and as sensory knowledge.

Finally this and other work on the senses provides a curious challenge for visual anthropology. Visual anthropologists have often acknowledged the existence of the anthropology of the senses. I have not encountered any resistance to the idea that visual anthropology should be engaging with non-visual sensory experience. However, as yet (with the exception of MacDougall's (e.g. 1998, 2001) and Ruby's (2000) arguments that film is an appropriate medium for the visual representation of sensory embodied experience) the subdiscipline has not taken this question on board. There has been some attention to the question of how one might use film to represent, by synaesthesia or metaphor, olfactory and tactile experience. However, the potential of audio-visual media (video and photography) for researching other people's sensory worlds has not been explored in existing work on visual anthropology research methodology. Attention to the senses and the notion of pluri-sensory experience that is represented and acted on through use of sensory metaphor invites anthropologists to think through the implications of their uses of visual methodologies in research and representation.

Conclusion

In this book I have offered an insight into the importance of sensory research for understanding a particular ethnographic context – the home – and a contemporary phenomena – changing gender. As an anthropological study of the senses in modern western culture and society this book is limited by its substantive focus. This is not simply a book about sensory experience but a project that treats the sensory home and sensory knowledge as fundamental aspects both of the research context – the home – and of the substantive concern of the research – changing gender. Undertaking this work has – along with my discovery of contemporary projects such as those of Desjarlais (2003) and Geurts (e.g. 2002) – convinced me that a more comprehensive engagement with sensory experience is important for anthropology. Works by Seremetakis (1994), Okely (1994), Stoller (1997), Ingold (2000) and MacDougall (1998), who have (albeit with slightly different emphases and arguments) generally taken a phenomenological and reflexive approach, also propose a reflexive anthropology that engages with the multi- or pluri-sensory nature of human experience. However, if anthropology is to account more fully for sensory aspects of our lives I suggest it needs to be open in two ways. First, open to learning from other disciplines. Ingold (2000) and MacDougall (1998), for instance, engage biological/medical accounts of vision and hearing and vision and touch respectively to develop their arguments. Nonetheless further interdisciplinary work could be done. Working in multi- or interdisciplinary teams on such themes could afford anthropologists important insights into scientifically constructed knowledge about sensory perception that might enhance our ability to analyse social and cultural aspects of sensory experience and practice. Second, anthropology needs to be open to new fieldwork methodologies and forms of representation. This might involve sensory workshops or performances, or more tangible products like hypermedia that combine film and writing.

Note

1. An exception is Cristina Grasseni (2004) whose notion of 'skilled vision' is developed in relation to Lave and Wenger's (1991) notion of a 'community of practice'.

Bibliography

Alberdi, I. (1999), *La nueva familia espanola*, Spain: Taurus.

Alborch, C. (1999), *Solas*, Madrid: Ediciones Temas de Hoy.

Amit, V. (1999), 'Introduction: Constructing the field', in V. Amit (ed.), *Constructing the Field*, London: Routledge.

—— (ed.) (2002), *Realising Community*, London: Routledge.

Anjar, M. (1999), 'Toys for Girls: Objects, Women and Memory in the Renaissance household', in M. Kwint, C. Breward and J. Aynsley (eds), *Material Memories: Design and Evocation*, Oxford: Berg.

Back, L. (1993), 'Gendered Participation: Masculinity and Fieldwork in a South London Adolescent Community', in D. Bell, P. Caplan and W. Jahan Karim (eds), *Gendered Fields: Women, Men and Ethnography*, London: Routledge.

Banks, M. (2001), *Visual Methods in Social Research*, London: Sage.

Beer, W. (1983), *Househusbands: Men and Housework in American Families*, New York: Praeger Publishers.

Berger, M., B. Wallis and S. Watson (1995), 'Introduction' in M. Berger, B. Wallis and S. Watson (eds), *Constructing Masculinity*, London: Routledge.

Birdwell-Pheasant, D. and D. Lawrence-Zúñiga (1999), 'Introduction: Houses and Families in Europe', in D. Birdwell-Pheasant and D. Lawrence-Zúñiga (eds), *House Life: Space, Place and Family in Europe*, Oxford: Berg.

Booth, S. (1999), 'Reconstructing Sexual Geography: Gender and Space in Changing Siclian Settlements', in D. Birdwell-Pheasant and D. Lawrence-Zúñiga (eds), *House Life: Space, Place and Family in Europe*, Oxford: Berg.

Borrell Velasco, V. (1992), 'Mujer y Vida Pública', in P. Sanchíz (ed.), *Mujer Andaluza: ¿la caída de un mito?,* Seville: Muñoz Moya Montraveta Editores.

Bourdieu, P. (1990), 'The Kabyle House or the World Reversed', in P. Bourdieu, *The Logic of Practice*, Cambridge: Polity.

—— (1998), 'Appendix: the Family Spirit', in P. Bowdien *Practical Reason*, Cambridge: Polity.

—— (1999), *Distinction: A Social Critique of the Judgement of Taste*, London: Routledge.

Brandes, S. (1981), 'Like Wounded Stags: Male Sexual Ideology in an Andalusian Town', in S. Ortner, and H. Whitehead, (eds), *Sexual Meanings: The Cultural Construction of Gender and Sexuality*, Cambridge: Cambridge University Press.

Brooksbank Jones, A. (1997), *Women in Contemporary Spain*, Manchester: Manchester University Press.

Bubandt, N. (1998), 'The Odour of Things: Smell and the Cultural Elaboration of Disgust in Eastern Indonesia', in *Ethnos*, 63 (1): 48–80.

Camas, V., A. Martinez and R. Munoz (2000), 'Hacia un modelo integrado de grupo de tarea-formación para la intervención: génesis, fundamentos y metodología del proyecto', in A. Martinez (ed.), *Taller de las Cuatro Estaciones: Viaje en torno al Deseo y la Mujer en la Identidad del Sur de Europa. Una aproximación socioantropológica*, Madrid: Urgel.

Carloni Franca, C. (1992), 'Macarena o como la conciencia llega a una muchacha de un corral de vecinos sevillano', in P. Sanchíz (ed.), *Mujer Andaluza: la caida de un mito?* Spain: Munoz Moya y Montraveta Editores, Biblioteca Andaluza

Catedra, M. ((ed.) 1991), *Los Españoles vistos por los antropólogos*, Madrid: Ediciones Júcar.

Chevalier, S. (1995), 'The Anthropology of an Apparent Banality: A Comparative Study', in *Cambridge Anthropology*, 19 (3).

—— (1998), 'From Woollen Carpet to Grass Carpet: Bridging House and Garden in an English Suburb', in D. Miller (ed.), *Material Cultures*, London: Routledge.

Clarke, A. (2001), 'The Aesthetics of Social Aspiration', in D. Miller (ed.), *Home Possessions*, Oxford: Berg.

—— (2002), 'Taste Wars and Design Dilemmas: Aesthetic Practice in the Home', in C. Painter (ed.), *Contemporary Art and the Home*, Oxford: Berg.

Classen, C. (1993), *Worlds of Sense: Exploring the Senses in History and Across Cultures*, London: Routledge.

——, D. Howes and A. Synnott (eds) (1994), *Aroma: The Cultural History of Smell*, London: Routledge.

Cohen, A. and N. Rapport (1995), *Questions of Consciousness*, London: Routledge.

Connell, R.W. (1987), *Gender and Power*, Cambridge: Polity Press.

—— (1995), *Masculinities*, Cambridge: Polity Press.

Cool, J. (1994), *Home Economics*, CVA, University of Southern California (ethnographic video).

Corbin, J. and M. Corbin (1984), *Compromising Relations: Kith, Kin and Class in Andalusia*, Hampshire, UK: Gower Publishing Company.

—— (1986), *Urbane Thought: Culture and Class in an Andalusian City*, Hampshire, UK: Gower Publishing Company.

Cornwall, A. and Lindisfarne, N. (1994a), 'Introduction', in A. Cornwall and N. Lindisfarne (eds), *Dislocating Masculinity: Comparative Ethnographies*, London: Routledge.

—— (1994b), 'Dislocating Masculinity: Gender, Power and Anthropology', in A. Cornwall and N. Lindisfarne (eds), *Dislocating Masculinity: Comparative Ethnographies*, London: Routledge.

—— (eds) (1994c), *Dislocating Masculinity: Comparative Ethnographies*, London: Routledge.

Cousins, C. (1994), 'A Comparison of the Labour Market Position of Women in Spain and the UK with Reference to the "Flexible" Labour Debate', in *Work, Employment and Society*, 8 (1): 45–67.

Craik, J. (1989), 'The Making of Mother', in G. Allan and G. Crow (eds), *Home and family*, London: Macmillan.

De Coppet, D. (1992), 'Comparison, a Universal for Anthropology: From "Re-presentation", to the Comparison of Hierarchies of Value', in A. Kuper (ed.), *Conceptualising Society*, London: Routledge.

Desjarlais, R. (2003), *Sensory Biographies: Lives and Deaths among Nepal's Yolmo Buddhists*, California: The University of California Press.

Dovey, K. (1999), *Framing Places*, London: Routledge.

Drazin, A. (2001), 'A Man *will* get Furnished: Wood and Domesticity in Urban Romania', in D. Miller (ed.), *Home Possessions*, Oxford: Berg.

Edwards, E. (1999), 'Photographs as Objects of Memory', in M. Kwint, C. Breward and J. Aynsley (eds), *Material Memories: Design and Evocation*, Oxford: Berg.

Emmison, M. and P. Smith (2000), *Researching the Visual*, London: Sage.

Englund, H. and J. Leach (2000), 'Ethnography and Meta-Narratives of Modernity', in *Current Anthropology*, 41: 225–48.

Feld, S. (1996), 'Waterfalls of Song: And Acoustemology of Place Resounding in Bosavi, Papua New Guinea', in S. Feld and K.H. Basso (eds), *Senses of Place*, Santa Fe: Schooll of American Research Press.

Fernandez, J. (1995), 'Amazing Grace: Meaning Deficit, Displacement and New Consciousness in Expressive Action', in A. Cohen and N. Rapport (eds), *Questions of Consciousness*, London: Routledge.

Finkel Morgenstein, L. (1997), *El reparto del trabajo domestico en la familia: la socialización en las diferencias del genero*, Madrid: CEAPA.

Garvey, P. (2001), 'Organised Disorder: Moving Furniture in Norwegian Homes', in D. Miller (ed.), *Home Possessions*, Oxford: Berg.

Geurts, K.L. (2002), 'On Rocks, Walks, and Talks in West Africa: Cultural Categories and an Anthropology of the Senses', in *Ethnos* 30 (3): 1–22.

Giddens, A. (1984), *The Constitution of Society*, Cambridge: Polity Press.

Gil Calvo, E. (1993), 'Mujeres. Asalto al Poder', in *El País Semanal*, no. 121, 13 June.

Gil Tebar, P. (1992), 'La reina de la casa en el tiempo infintio', in P. Sanchíz (ed.), *Mujer Andaluza: la caida de un mito?*, Spain: Munoz Moya y Montraveta Editores, Biblioteca Andaluza.

Gilmore, D. (1985), 'Introduction', in D. Gilmore (ed.), *Sex and Gender in Southern Europe: Problems and Prospects,* Special Issue no. 3 of *Anthropology*, May–December, 4 (1–2).

—— (1987), *Aggression and Community: Paradoxes of Andalusian Culture*, New Haven: Yale University Press.

—— (1990), *Manhood in the Making: Cultural Concepts of Masculinity,* New Haven: Yale University Press.

Goddard, V. (1994), 'From the Mediterranean to Europe: Honour, Kinship and Gender', in V. Goddard, J.R. Llobera and C. Shore (eds), *The Anthropology of Europe: Identities and Boundaries in Conflict*, Oxford: Berg.

—— (2000), 'Introduction', in V. Goddard (ed.), *Gender, Agency and Change: Anthropological Perspectives*, London: Routledge.

Grasseni, C. (2004), 'Video and Ethnographic Knowledge: Skilled Vision in the Practice of Breeding', in S. Pink, L. Kurti, and A.I. Afonso (eds) (2004), *Working Images*, London: Routledge.

Grimshaw, A. (2001), *The Ethnographer's Eye*, Cambridge: Cambridge University Press.

Gullestad, M. (1993), 'Home Decoration as Popular Culture. Constructing Homes, Genders and Classes in Norway', in T. de Valle (ed.), *Gendered Anthropology*, London: Routledge,

Gupta, A. and J. Ferguson (1997), 'Introduction', in A. Gupta and J. Ferguson (eds), *Culture, Power, Place*, Durham: Duke University Press.

Halle, D. (1993), *Inside Culture: Art and Class in the American Home*, Chicago: University of Chicago Press.

Harris, O. (1996), 'The Temporalities of Tradition: Reflections on a Changing Anthropology', in V. Hubinger (ed.), *Grasping the Changing World*, London: Routledge.

Hart, A. (1994), 'Missing Masculinity?: Prostitutes' Clients in Alicante, Spain', in A. Cornwall and N. Lindisfarne (eds), *Dislocating*

Masculinity: Comparative Ethnographies, London: Routledge.

Hecht, A. (2001), 'Home Sweet Home: Tangible Memories of an Uprooted Childhood', in D. Miller (ed.), *Home Possessions*, Oxford: Berg.

Holliday, R. (2000), 'We've Been Framed: Visualising Methodology', in *The Sociological Review*, 48 (4): 503–22.

Horsfield, M. (1998), *Biting the Dust: The Joys of Housework*, London: Fourth Estate Limited.

Hoskins, J. (1998), *Biographical Objects: How Things Tell the Stories of People's Lives*, London: Routledge.

Howes, D. (1991), 'Sensorial Anthropology', in D. Howes (ed.), *The Varieties of Sensory Experience: A Sourcebook in the Anthropology of the Senses*, Toronto: University of Toronto Press.

Hughes-Freeland, F. (1998), 'Introduction' in F. Hughes-Freeland (ed.), *Ritual, Performance, Media*, London: Routledge.

—— (2004), 'Working Images: Conclusion', in S. Pink, L. Kurti and A.I. Afonso (eds), *Working Images*, London: Routledge.

Ingold, T. (2000), *The Perception of the Environment: Essays in Livelihood, Dwelling and Skill*, London: Routledge.

James, W., J. Hockey and A. Dawson (1997), *After Writing Culture*, London: Routledge.

Kulick, D. (1995), 'Introduction: The Sexual Life of Anthropologists: Erotic Subjectivity and Ethnographic Work', in D. Kulick and M. Willson (eds), *Taboo: Sex, Identity and Erotic Subjectivity in Anthropological Fieldwork*, London: Routledge.

—— and M Willson (eds) (1995), *Taboo: Sex, Identity and Erotic Subjectivity in Anthropological Fieldwork*, London: Routledge.

Kuper, A. (1999), *Culture: The Anthropologists' Account*, Cambridge: Harvard University Press.

Lave, J. and E. Wenger (1991), *Situated Learning: Legitimate Peripheral Participation*, Cambridge: Cambridge University Press.

Loizos, P. (1992), 'User-Friendly Ethnography?', in J. da Pina Cabral and J. Campbell (eds), *Europe Observed: Anthropological Fieldwork in Southern Europe*, London: Macmillan.

Lutkehaus, N. and J. Cool (1999), 'Paradigms Lost and Found: The "Crisis of Representation" and Visual Anthropology', in J.M. Gaines and M. Renov (eds), *Collecting Visible Evidence*, Minneapolis: University of Minnesota Press.

MacClancey, J. (1996), 'Female Bullfighting, Gender Stereotyping and the State', in J. MacClancey (ed.), *Sport, identity and Ethnicity*, Oxford: Berg.

MacDougall, D. (1997), 'The Visual in Anthropology', in M. Banks and

154 • Bibliography

H. Morphy (eds), *Rethinking Visual Anthropology*, New Haven: Yale University Press.

—— (1998), *Transcultural Cinema*, Princeton: Princeton University Press.

—— (2000), 'Social Aesthetics and The Doon School', in *Sights* http://cc.joensuu.fi/sights/david2.htm.

—— (2001), 'Renewing Ethnographic Film: Is Digital Video Changing the Genre?', in Anthropology Today 17 (3): 51–21.

Malos, E. (1995), 'The Politics of Household Labour in the 1990s', in E. Malos (ed.), *The Politics of Housework* (new edition), Cheltenham: New Clarion Press.

Marcoux, J. (2001), 'The Refurbishment of Memory', in D. Miller (ed.), *Home Possessions*, Oxford: Berg.

Marcus, G. (1995), 'The Modernist Sensibility in Recent Ethnographic Writing and the Cinematic Metaphor of Montage', in L. Devereaux and R. Hillman (eds), *Fields of Vision*, Berkeley: University of California Press.

Martinez, A. (ed.) (2000), *Taller de las Cuatro Estaciones: Viaje en torno al Deseo y la Mujer en la Identidad del Sur de Europa. Una aproximación socioantropológica*, Madrid: Urgel.

——, J. Consigny, M. Lorenzo, M. Cerezo, M. Ortiz, P. Lopez, R. Muñoz and V. Camas (2000), *Mujeres Invisibles*, Taller de Antropología Visual, Madrid (ethnographic video).

Massey, D. (1998), 'Blurring the Binaries?: High-tech in Cambridge', in R. Ainley (ed.), *New Frontiers of Space, Bodies and Gender*, London: Routledge.

McElhinny, B. (1994), 'An Economy of Affect: Objectivity, Masculinity and the Gendering of Police Work', in A. Cornwall and N. Lindisfarne (eds), *Dislocating Masculinity: Comparative Ethnographies*, London: Routledge.

McHugh, K. (1997), 'One Cleans, the Other Doesn't', in *Cultural Studies*, 11 (1): 17–39.

Merleau Ponty, M. (1992), *Phenomenology of Perception*, London: Routledge.

Miel, G. (1997), 'La redefinicion de la division de trabajo domestico en la nueva familia urbana espanola', in *Reis* 80 (97): 69–93.

Miller, D. (1988), 'Appropriating the State on the Council Estate', in *Man*, 23: 353–72.

—— (ed.) (1998a), *Material Cultures*, London: Routledge.

—— (1998b), 'Why Some Things Matter', in D. Miller (ed.), *Material Cultures*, London: Routledge.

—— (2001a), 'Behind Closed Doors', in D. Miller (ed.) *Home*

Possessions, Oxford: Berg.

—— (2001b), 'Possessions', in D. Miller (ed.) *Home Possessions*, Oxford: Berg.

—— (2002), 'Accomodating', in C. Painter (ed.), *Contemporary Art and the Home*, Oxford: Berg.

Moore, H. (1993), 'The Differences Within and the Differences Between', in T. de Valle (ed.), *Gendered Anthropology*, London: Routledge.

—— (1994), *A Passion for Difference*, Cambridge: Polity Press.

—— (1999a), 'Anthropology at the Turn of the Century', in H. Moore (ed.), *Anthropological Theory Today*, Cambridge: Polity Press.

—— (1999b), 'Gender and other crises in anthropology', in H. Moore (ed.), *Anthropological Theory Today*, Cambridge: Polity Press.

Morley, D. (2000), *Home Territories: Media, Mobility and Identity*, London: Routledge.

Morris, R. (1995), 'ALL MADE UP: Performance Theory and the New Anthropology of Sex and Gender', in *Annual Review of Anthropology*, 24: 567–92.

Oakley, A. (1974 [1985]), *The Sociology of Housework*, Oxford: Basil Blackwell.

Okely, J. (1994), Vicarious and Sensory Knowledge of Chronology and Change: Ageing in Rural France', in K. Hastrup and P. Hervik (eds), *Social Experience and Anthropological Knowledge*, London: Routledge.

—— (1996), *Own or Other Culture*, London: Routledge.

Ortner, S. and H. Whitehead (1981), *Sexual Meanings: The Cultural Construction of Gender and Sexuality*, Cambridge: Cambridge University Press.

Pahl, R. (2000), *On Friendship*, Oxford: Polity Press.

Petridou, E. (2001), 'The Taste of Home', in D. Miller (ed.), *Home Possessions*, Oxford: Berg.

Pink, S. (1997a), *Women and Bullfighting: Gender, Sex and the Consumption of Tradition*, Oxford: Berg.

—— (1997b), 'Female Bullfighters, Festival Queens in the Dole Queue, and Women Who Want to Fly: Gender, Tradition, Change and Work in Andalusia', in *Self, Agency and Society*, 1 (2).

—— (1999), '"Informants" who come "Home"', in V. Amit (ed.), *Constructing the Field*, London: Routledge.

—— (2000), 'Men with Mops, Women with Swords: Changing Spanish Gender Identities', in *Thompson Learning Anthropology* at www.anthro-online.com.

—— (2001), *Doing Visual Ethnography: Images, Media and Representation in Research*, London: Sage.

—— (2003a), 'Representing the Sensory Home: Ethnographic Experience and Ethnographic Hypermedia', in G. Bloustien (ed.), *Envisioning Ethnography: Exploring the Complexity of the Visual Methods in Ethnographic research, Social Analysis*, 47 (3): 46–53.

—— (2003b), '"She Wasn't Tall Enough and Breasts Get in the Way": Why Would a Woman Bullfighter Retire?', in *Identities: Global Studies in Culture and Power*.

—— (2004), 'Conversing Anthropologically: Hypermedia as Anthropological Text', in S. Pink, L. Kurti and A.I. Afonso (eds), *Working Images*, London: Routledge.

—— (forthcoming), 'Applications of Anthropology: Introduction', in S. Pink (ed.), *Applications of Anthropology*, Oxford: Berghahn.

Pitt-Rivers, J. (1963), *The People of the Sierra*, Chicago: University of Chicago Press.

Rapport, N. (1997), *Transcendent Individual*, London: Routledge.

—— (1998), 'Hard Sell: Commercial Performance and the Narration of Self', in F. Hughes-Freeland (ed.), *Ritual, Performance, Media*, London: Routledge.

—— and A.Dawson (1998b), 'Home and Movement: A Polemic', in N. Rapport and A. Dawson, *Migrants of Identity*, Oxford: Berg.

—— and Dawson, A. (1998c), 'The Topic and the Book', in N. Rapport and A. Dawson, *Migrants of Identity*, Oxford: Berg.

—— and J. Overing (2000), *Social and Cultural Anthropology: The Key Concepts*, London: Routledge.

Renov, M. (1999), 'Domestic Ethnography and the Construction of the "Other" Self', in J.M. Gaines and M. Renov (eds), *Collecting Visible Evidence*, Minneapolis: University of Minnesota Press.

Rice, T. (2003), 'Soundselves: An Acoustemology of Sound and Self in the Edinburgh Royal Infirmary', in *Anthropology Today*, 19 (4): 4–9.

Rose, G. (2001), *Visual Methodologies*, London: Sage.

Rostas, S. (1998), 'From Ritualisation to Performativity: the Concheros of Mexico', in F. Hughes-Freeland (ed.), *Ritual, Performance, Media*, London: Routledge.

Ruby, J. (2000), *Picturing Culture: Explorations of Film and Anthropology*, Chicago: University of Chicago Press.

Sanchíz, P. (ed.), (1992), *Mujer Andaluza: la caida de un mito?*, Spain: Munoz Moya y Montraveta Editores, Biblioteca Andaluza.

Sanders, R. (1998), *The Social Construction of Domestic Space in Cordoba, Andalusia (Spain)*, University of Kent at Canterbury, UK, PhD thesis in Social Anthropology.

Schieffelin, E. (1998), 'Problematizing Performance', in F. Hughes-Freeland (ed.), *Ritual, Performance, Media*, London: Routledge.

Seremetakis, L. (1994), 'The memory of the Senses: Historical Perception, Commensal Exchange, and Modernity', in L. Taylor (ed.), *Visualizing Theory*, London: Routledge.

Seymour, J. (1992), '"Its Not a Manly Thing to do": Gender Accountability and the Division of Domestic Labour', in G.A. Dunne, R.M. Blackburn and J. Jarman (eds), *Inequalities in Employment, Inequalities in Home-Life*, Conference Proceedings for the 20th Cambridge Social Stratification Seminar, University of Cambridge.

Shove, E. (2003), *Comfort, Cleanliness and Convenience: The Social Organisation of Normality*, Oxford: Berg.

Silva, E. (2000), 'The Politics of Consumption @ Home', PAVIS Papers in Social and Cultural Research, Number 1, Faculty of Social Sciences, The Open University.

Sobchack, V. (1992), *The Address of the Eye*, Princeton: Princeton University Press.

Social Trends, available at <http://www.statistics.gov.uk/default.asp>

Spinella, M. (2002), 'A Relationship between Smell Identification and Empathy', in *International Journal of Neuroscience*, 112: 605–12.

Stewart, S. (1999), 'Prologue: From the Museum of Touch', in M. Kwint, C. Breward and J. Aynsley (eds), *Material Memories: Design and Evocation*, Oxford: Berg.

Stoller, P. (1989), *The Taste of Ethnographic Things: The Senses in Ethnography*, Philadelphia: University of Pennsylvania Press.

—— (1997), *Sensuous Scholarship*, Philadelphia: University of Pennsylvania Press.

Strathern, M. (1981), *Kinship at the Core: An Anthropology of Elmdon, Essex*, Cambridge: Cambridge University Press

—— (1992), 'Parts and Wholes: Refiguring Relationships in a Post-Plural World', in A. Kuper (ed.), *Conceptualising Society*, London: Routledge.

—— (1993), 'Making Incomplete', in V. Broche-Due, I. Rudie and T. Bleie (eds), *Carved Flesh Cast Selves: Gendered Symbols and Social Practices*, Oxford: Berg.

Sullivan, O. (2000), 'The Division of Domestic Labour: 20 Years of Change?', in *Sociology*, 34 (3): 437–56.

—— (forthcoming), 'Gender Transformations Within the Household: Some Kinds of Change are Slow', in *Gender and Society.*

Tacchi, J. (1998), 'Radio Texture: Between Self and Others', in D. Miller (ed.), *Material Cultures*, London: Routledge.

Taussig, M. (1991), 'Tactility and Distraction', in *Cultural Anthropology*, 6: 147–53.

—— (1993), *Mimesis and Alterity: A Particular Study of the Senses*, London: Routledge.

Taylor, L. (ed.) (1994), *Visualizing Theory*, London: Routledge.

Thuren, B. (2000), 'Out of the house – to do what? Women in the Spanish neighbourhood movement', in V. Goddard (ed.), *Gender, Agency and Change: Anthropological Perspectives,* London: Routledge.

Tulloch, J. (1999), *Performing Culture*, London: Sage.

Wenger, E., R. McDermott, W. Snyder (2002), *Cultivating Communities of Practice, A guide to Managing Knowledge*, Boston: Harvard Business School Press.

West, C. and D.H. Zimmerman (1991[1987]), 'Doing Gender', in *Gender and Society* 1: 125–51.

Wilk, R. (1999), 'Towards a Useful Theory of Consumption', *European Council for an Energy Efficient Economy Summer Study Proceedings*, Paris: ADEME.

Zambrano, B. (1999), *Solas* (feature film).

Index